I CRIED OUT,
YOU ANSWERED ME

By SHEREE MCMILLEN

Published by
Spiritbuilding Publishing
15591 N. State Rd. 9
Summitville, IN 46070

Spiritual "equipment" for the contest of life.

Printed in the United States of America

ACKNOWLEDGEMENTS

Dealing with the events occurring in 2006 left me analyzing not only the events leading up to my husband's breakdown, but my life in general. Now analyzing is something that I do, **a lot**. I don't know why, I just do. And as I was performing my analysis, it caused me to reflect on why I reacted and handled situations as I did during Bart's intense struggle. I have never before been in a position like I was in 2006. Critical decisions concerning the help and medical attention for another person were mine. I was the one in control, calling the shots. I had help and support, but ultimately Bart's health and future was up to me. With that responsibility came a level of fear and a greater dependence on God. Aware of the results that I wanted to see, my focus became clear, precise, and unwavering. I didn't know how we were going to get there, but I knew where we were going and I knew that God was the only way it could happen.

One way that I feel that God provided for us was in the support group that we had. To these precious people, I am forever grateful. This is something that I highly recommend to anyone who might find themselves in a similar situation. Turn to those you can trust. Typically, I am a very independent person. I will do it myself if I can, and if I can't, it is then that I ask for help. Don't try to do it by yourself because you can't. It is imperative that you seek those you can trust for help and support. You are not alone nor are you the first person to ever face a situation like yours, and the sooner that you accept it, the sooner you and your loved one will be on the road to recovery—albeit a long road, but the right road.

I was concerned about sharing the details of Bart's condition which caused me to be very protective of him. I was careful to keep him and the details of his condition from those who would take advantage of his vulnerability. I have never been embarrassed that Bart had a nervous breakdown. I was heartbroken that he was suffering. Regardless of how frustrated I would be with him sometimes, I was always aware of preserving his dignity. Bart was so misunderstood by so many, including me, but I knew that I was the one setting the tone on the perception of Bart and that I would be much more forgiving of him than others. If I was leaving an image of Bart with anyone, I wanted it to be one that was preserving his dignity. This is one of the reasons that I only confided in a few; also because I didn't have time to consult with a large number of people. Bart was requiring so much of my time, as well as all of the typical responsibilities that come with being the mother of three small children.

I only shared our situation with a handful of people who weren't medical professionals. They each played a significant role in this ordeal, and without these people and the prayers of so many, we would not have made it. Our support system included Sherry Rickard, one of my best friends from high school, Sarah Beutelschies, my aunt, Bruce and Rachel Reeves, local friends, and R. L. and Patsy McMillen, Bart's parents.

Sherry's role was a supportive sounding board. She lives a few hours away with her own family which did not allow her the opportunity to be in Conway. This didn't matter because the role that she played was exactly what was needed.

Sarah is also one who does not live in Conway, but provided necessary support and encouragement. Being only eight years older than me, Sarah has always been more like a sister. I have always adored her. She is very positive, proactive, and plan-oriented. She helped to keep my thinking straight during this time. I have always trusted Sherry and Sarah. They had our best interest at heart, and I desperately needed a support group in order to share the circumstances. Even though they weren't involved with the ins and outs of the daily struggle, the importance of their role was without measure.

Bruce and Rachel live in Conway, and Bruce preaches at the local church where we attend services. They are also very good friends of ours. Not only were they sounding boards for us, they also played an essential role in the process of Bart's recovery. These two were responsible for me keeping my sanity. They were available 24/7 and directly involved with the ins and outs of our life at this time, and believe me, we needed them.

The other two making up our support group were Bart's parents. They provided support and confidence for me which meant more than I can ever express. They have always had an active role in Bart's life and in our life since Bart and I began seeing each other. They don't meddle or pry, and their family is their life. With the circumstances being as they were with Bart and his condition, they never tried to take over. They consulted me. They honored my requests and supported my decisions. There were times when I would have to deal with just one of them because of the communication loop. With more than two people involved, communication can become sketchy, and quite honestly I don't prefer communicating this way. I prefer direct communication. I am clear in where I stand, and at a time like this there was no time for any additional confusion.

As we began the uphill climb following the crash, I found that there were specific individuals best suited for specific areas of repair. My father-in-law was who I worked with concerning the business because he had been one of the partners in the original business with Bart. There were financial issues to address which required his help. He was also a big help when it came to dealing with Bart's emotional state. It was after Bart's emotional state became moderately balanced that my mother-in-law was most instrumental. Once all of the information was shared and Bart felt safe that our relationship was not in jeopardy, he became more active in turning the situation around.

I would also like to acknowledge our three wonderful children. I am forever grateful for them and what they bring to my life. They are responsible for providing me with one of my most treasured roles in life—motherhood. I could go on and on about them but this is not the time or the place. So what I would like to say is that they were one of the most important reasons that I fought so hard for Bart's recovery. My children deserve their dad. They love him and they need him. There were so many times that it was their sweet little faces, happy or sad, dirty or clean, that kept me going. They motivate and encourage me in so many ways that they will never know.

So from the bottom of my heart, I want to thank you. You all are truly special people, instrumental in not only ensuring that our family stay intact, but that we recover much stronger than when we began this struggle. Each of you is a very special gift in our lives and we love you. Also, to those of you who have had us in your prayers, we thank you. And just so you know, prayer works. Don't ever stop.

Contents

Chapter 1
FROM ME TO YOU

I share my story with you as the caregiver of someone who suffered a nervous breakdown while battling depression in the hopes of providing you with a source of encouragement when you find yourself in a difficult time. You are not alone. You are not the first to be in this position, and you won't be the last. When we were struggling through this ordeal, I earnestly desired to seek out caregivers of similar situations. There were those who had shared their story of suffering depression and the horrors that entailed, but there were no accounts from any caregivers—no outlines for those trying to help a loved one in trouble. It is because of this that I share with you the things that I did for my husband, Bart. I am in no way an expert on depression and do not claim to be. I am simply a wife and mother who found herself in a tough situation. I found myself relying on prayer, instinct, support of loved ones, and my love for Bart. I love Bart, and I love my children. They are my heart and soul, and they are worth it. Because you have those in your life who mean the same to you, I hope that this account gives you courage, hope, and support.

Depression is a mean disease that knows no boundaries. Regardless of what may be the culprit, the variable of stress is always involved. Now I could go on and on about how I believe that a healthy lifestyle which is centered on maintaining a balance in our mind, body, and spirit is crucial as a defense for depression. This is an excellent idea as a preventative measure, but I must emphasize **preventative**. It is a completely different ballgame when depression strikes. Survival becomes the game plan and healthy lifestyle is out the window, temporarily.

Some of the things that I learned while experiencing this time with Bart I would like to share with you now.

- During a time like this, I think growth is inevitable. I found it best to not only accept it, but embrace it.
- Our attitude is just as important at a time of crisis as it is on a daily basis. It is what dictates progression.
- Sometimes where we find ourselves is not at all where we intended to land.

- Things aren't always what they appear to be.
- You have a choice. The options aren't always what you would prefer, but you do have a choice.
- To be fair means to be fair to you as well. I am not referring to sacrifices made to care for your loved one. If this is your spouse, this is a commitment that you made in your vows. I am referring to those things which deal with you preserving your self-respect. I am not speaking of all health conditions or types of abuse. I am referring to depression only, and a depressed person still knows right from wrong. You have to remember that in order for your loved one to heal and your relationship to survive, you must command the respect for yourself that you show to others. This includes your loved one. Sacrifice for another does not mean that you are to eliminate your values and the respect that you deserve. This is what you pull from in order to help another. Don't lose yourself and who you are to this situation too. This isn't helping your loved one. At a time like this, you can't afford to become a casualty. Taking care of you is essential to providing the best care for others. Think of this in terms of boundaries. They are necessary in order to develop healthy relationships, and to sacrifice essentials such as boundaries sets up a scenario for future problems. I believe in boundaries. And for me at this time I knew that I didn't want to be back in this position again. I was willing to learn what I needed to learn, and boundaries would help to preserve what we had and completely heal in the process.
- Trust yourself. Do the best you can with what you have. Make your decision and don't look back.

When Bart and I married, we committed to each other wholeheartedly, without reservation. We have often talked about this and how we both felt that we were made for each other. This does not mean that we take our relationship for granted. In fact, it is quite the opposite. We hold our relationship in high regard with supreme priority. We are best friends who hold the greatest respect for each other. Are we perfect? Oh no. Not even close. We are, however, perfect for each other because we want to be. We intend to be.

Our honeymoon in Cancun

Loving Bart is not work. Life is work. For us marriage is the united front we use to face life. Some of the aspects upon which our relationship is based are honesty, trust, and communication. As a result, when Bart crashed, each of these aspects of our relationship were truly tested, which rocked the very core of our relationship. Fortunately, we are both tenaciously loyal and determined or the outcome of this situation could have occurred so differently.

For me, being the caregiver to one suffering from depression brought about so many emotions, and I found that I was not at liberty to express them in Bart's presence because of how fragile his condition had become. An analogy that I would use to describe this time would be a slot machine. When the handle is pulled, the emotions would be spinning and often blur together. When the spinning stopped, the emotion on which the wheel stopped was the emotion that was expressed. Otherwise, the emotions were constantly swirling. I had no control of when the wheel started or stopped. A few of the most prominent emotions that I experienced in large proportions were the following.

Loneliness

Loneliness was apparent for me soon after Bart crashed. This was the first time in our relationship that it felt that Bart and I were not united in dealing with life's challenges. I actually found myself having to function as a single parent because Bart was simply unable to perform in that capacity. He required more attention and care than our three small children. This was a time when I needed him so desperately. I needed his help, his support, and his strength. I needed Bart.

Hurt

Bart's crash not only hurt him, but it hurt me too. It hurt to my very core to see him struggle with the simplest of routine tasks. It hurt to see him cry. It hurt to not be able to cry in front of him because of how it would affect him. It hurt to know that he was so scared and so hurt and I couldn't change it. It hurt to see him so fragile.

Fear

I was scared. One of my biggest fears is something happening to Bart. I would lose my best friend and be left to raise our children alone. I don't ever allow myself to think of this because it terrifies me. When he crashed, this was thrown right in my face. This fear was so closely a reality and I knew it. But with that being said, I didn't focus on it. What I did focus on was getting Bart as far away from that as possible. Everything that I did was in that direction. I was so scared that if he didn't move forward regardless of how slow, we were in danger. From the time that I would wake Bart in the morning until we would go to bed at night, I would not allow him to go back to bed. I know this sounds harsh, but he rested in the recliner if he needed to rest, and actually he preferred to lie on his stomach on the floor in his office. I was just afraid that if he ever allowed himself to go back to bed, that he would never get up. For me, Bart going to bed in this state would be the beginning of the end.

Sadness

I was so sad. The reality that we really have no idea what tomorrow holds was so prevalent. It felt as if our whole world had been turned upside down, and I had no idea if Bart and I would ever be the same.

Anger

I had so much anger. I was angry because at this point in time, it appeared that Bart was being dishonest with me and that he just continued to do so. I was angry with all of the confusion related to his business. I was angry that this confusion had now become my problem.

Love

Throughout it all, I loved Bart. I loved us and what we had. I wanted so badly for it to be ok. I loved our family, and I was determined to see this through. At times I would see glimpses of the Bart that I knew and loved. Those were encouraging and they helped. I would like to say that Bart is free of depression, never to deal with it again, but we all know that that is untrue and unrealistic. Bart no longer suffers with depression at that magnitude; he does, however, manage life as we all should—one day at a time. He is not a depressed person. He is a better person, a stronger person for enduring this challenge and seeing it through. With it he has allowed himself the opportunity to grow as only one can when challenges arise. Sometimes we must fall to the bottom so that we may place both feet firmly beneath our self and spring upward. Bart has done it. He is soaring upward. With all that this condition brought to his life, I think that he would quickly tell you that it was a blessing, and he chooses to see it that way. Not only is he stronger and more confident, we are stronger as a couple.

I admire him and I am so very proud of him. He could have allowed this situation to become prolonged and overtake him completely. He didn't. He did have help. I have always said that you can only help someone as much as they will help themselves. Bart had the desire. It was buried deep within, but it was there, and that is what made the difference.

Chapter 2
THE DAY

I remember the morning very clearly. I had the flu and had slept in a bit. This particular strand of the flu would endure for approximately two weeks. I was not quite mid-way through, however I was too far along to take Tamiflu to limit the extent of the discomfort. Needless to say, it was one mean bug and I was feeling bad.

I awoke to find Bart, my mother-in-law, and my children at the kitchen table. Bart had already planned to work from home and watch the kids. (Bart is a land surveyor and has his office at home.) So the surprise was not to see Bart that morning. The surprise was to see my mother-in-law, who is a school teacher, at our house on a school day and the expression on Bart's face as I entered the room. Every eye was on me as I entered the room. The mood was not typical. It was unsettling to say the least. I knew instantly that something big was going on. It was the feeling you have when you can sense that something bad has happened and everyone around knows but you. It was as if I was about to be told and the audience was waiting for a reaction. It had to be obvious that I was confused. Bart stood slowly and said that he wanted to talk to me. We went to the bedroom so that we could talk privately.

What I did not know at this time was that he had so many bills due without the money to pay them. He had surveys to do and collect from with no help at the time. Obviously, he was feeling helpless. This situation was not an isolated incident or just a slow time. This was a game that he had been playing for quite some time due in part to the way that his business had been set-up.

I realize that a question you may have is where was his wife during all of this? Well, I was there, but obviously not on top of Bart's developing condition. First of all, depression creeps in slowly acclimating those closest to the victim in a very subtle manner. Looking back I am able to recognize so many of the symptoms. But during the time leading to the breakdown, any behavior or symptom that was significant could be accounted elsewhere, leaving the rest to simply be accepted as a way of life.

I knew that Bart was under a lot of stress with his job. Surveying is what he loves to do and chose as a profession. He is one of the best. Along with that, it was his passion, not mine. This is not to say that I am not interested in surveying. I am interested in anything that Bart attempts. However, at the time, I didn't have a responsibility in the business so I didn't dig into the details. Not being one to interfere and already having significant obligations limiting my free time, I simply trusted him. When I would talk to Bart about bills, money, or whatever related to that, he would tell me that he was taking care of it, or would take care of it, or even his plan on collection. This is my downfall which has been there since Bart and I began dating. I believe him even beyond common sense. Even though there were times when I was not completely convinced, I always chose to believe him. I had and still do have faith in him. I wanted it for him.

Bart is not an extravagant spender, nor is he one who is afraid of taking a chance. His spending habits would involve only spending when he had the money to pay for it. After we were married, Bart charged a pin plotter for survey drawings on a credit card. He was so nervous and had the card paid off almost immediately. He was always very cautious about spending. I see now that cautious spending was his way of managing money. This was rather effective until he had established his business and he had some clients who failed to pay in a timely manner or simply not at all. This is when some of the problems began to manifest themselves. Over time this feast or famine type collection and "catch-up" money management began to rule the business. It was then that Bart became what seemed to be rather carefree, but was actually so frustrated and would spend without regard of consequences. This should have been a red flag for me, but I am sad to say that it was not, largely because of the reasons I just mentioned.

I want to make it clear that where Bart ended up was not where he set out to be. Of course, no one would ever say that they want a nervous breakdown. No one ever plans to have one. The point that I would like to make is that everyone should be planning with prevention. We are all simply one step away from the path to depression if we are not already almost there. We can all say that we know someone who has/had depression or have experienced ourselves some type of depression that was more than just "the blues." Most of us can list the many anti-depressants prescribed because they are so common. Depression is a part of our lives.

Now back to the morning --- Bart began telling me that he called his mother to ask her to come and help with the kids. He said that he had a dream that he tried to kill himself and he woke up scared. Bart was obviously shaken. As I was listening to him, I was trying to process what I was hearing. I had never before seen Bart like this, and I have never been close to anyone who was in this condition. Bart talked about how sick he had felt. He hadn't been able to eat or sleep. He told me that he was scared to sleep. He went into a few details about the debt. I was aware of the collection problem. Since he has been in this business, survey work and collection is typically slow prior to the holidays and extends through the beginning of the year. I also knew that Bart had been under more stress throughout the past year and that he had been recently struggling more than usual.

Bart's appearance was changing rapidly. It had begun before this particular day and was beginning to gain momentum that would continue in the months that followed. Obviously Bart was not all smiles on this particular day, but Bart is typically one who smiles easily with a large and often adolescent sense of humor. Actually, Bart hadn't smiled easily in some time, and it would be months before his humor would return. As Bart was sitting there on the sofa, he was so fragile. He desperately wanted all of this to go away, and he felt so helpless. He was reaching out to me and very much wanted me to understand and I didn't. I was trying to process this information based on the information that had been provided.

Typically, when I am faced with a serious situation, I am slow to react. I must process the information before coming to a possible solution or conclusion. I will analyze it to death. This process began when I woke up this particular morning. My head was swimming. I was running a temperature from the flu. I couldn't stand or sit erect for any length of time without feeling dizzy and nauseous. I was processing this experience with Bart in a physically compromised state, and I must admit I didn't even begin to realize the magnitude of this situation which had absolutely nothing to do with me having the flu.

As I said before, Bart is self-employed. So often I had written off the stress as part of the job. We had talked on various occasions about his work and possibly working for someone as opposed to continuing the role of self-employment or working for someone along with continuing his own business. Bart consistently desired to maintain his current position as business owner. In my heart, I knew that Bart was determined to come out on top in regard to his business, and I was not going to be yet another obstacle for him. With that being said, I was supportive of his decision, and I would encourage him to pursue avenues which would possibly enhance his knowledge of the business.

The conversations that we had throughout the day were just like the conversations that we had two weeks and four weeks prior. This was obviously not a new discussion and to me was becoming a bit frustrating due to the physical state that I was in during this most recent exchange. In my opinion, we had already settled the issues. We had come to the same conclusions each time. Bart was set to continue as a business owner. What I was not seeing and was not privy to until well beyond this day was the true root of this problem.

As the day progressed, Bart and I began putting a pen to paper. As I write this, I don't want to imply that this was a meeting of the minds with active participation from both parties. This was an all day process. Bart possessed a blank, lost look to his appearance. He was emotional at different times during the day. Bart and I began repeating the same conversations from the past; however, this time I moved on to a more active role which I maintained well beyond this particular day. I began listing his options, and he made his decision. (Same as before.) We then went on to make some plans which would actively improve his business. By nightfall we had moved to establishing a sense of organization to Bart's world. Time management has never been a strong point for Bart; however, this had reached an all time low. He was unable to focus on a task. I understand more now than I did at the time. Bart's mind had shut-down, which was in turn having a direct impact on not only his physical health and appearance but everything about him.

Looking back, I knew then that the situation was bad, but I had only one focus. The focus was Bart. I feel that I can accurately compare it to a major tragedy where those involved are functioning on pure adrenaline—the fight or flight syndrome. When a person finds themselves in tragedy, survival of those who are struggling is the only focus. True priorities rise to the top. There is no time to dwell on fear or "what-ifs." I was so focused on Bart getting better. I don't know if I could not or would not deviate from this course, but for whatever reason I didn't. I just felt that I had been brought to this moment in time because I could do whatever it took to "fix it." I am not claiming that I had all of the answers, and when the situation presented itself, I simply donned my gear and went to work like some super woman—if it were only that easy.

What I did have was a peace that God was with me. I was confident in my abilities only because I had faith in God. I didn't have the answers, but I did know where to go—**Prayer**. I knew without a doubt that I had been brought to this moment in time because God had a plan.

I knew that Bart's future, health, well-being, character, and dignity were dependent upon me. Our family was experiencing strains. I felt the burden fall on me and I was alone. I didn't have Bart fully in all capacities as a spouse, and this I sorely missed. Needless to say, I felt the pressure, and I wasn't willing to give up without a fight. I was fiercely determined. This was the only mode for me for the next several months.

Before we went to sleep that night, Bart and I made a list for the following day. He desperately needed some focus, direction, and help with time management. The list was comprised of only four "things to do." It was a rather simple list for anyone in a healthy mental state, but for Bart at this time, it was Mount Everest. After we completed the list, he looked a bit relieved. We had made some decisions for the future and the following day. We had a plan.

Bart's demeanor throughout the day was emotional and fearful. He had been losing weight without effort so his face looked thinner, but his eyes were sad and blank at the same time. His face appeared so hollow. He complained of physical pain. He wasn't very specific about where he hurt. He would just say that he hurt or that it was bad. This was a typical example of his responses throughout this battle with depression. Whenever I would ask Bart specifics about anything, he would respond with vague answers or what became his most popular—"I don't know." It took some time before I came to understand that he really didn't know. I will explain that more later.

My thoughts that night as we went to bed were only one thing. I had to get Bart out of bed in the morning. In my mind, the first and biggest hurdle that we were facing was keeping him out of bed. I was very afraid that if he were given the opportunity to simply hide in bed from whatever this was, it would only get worse. I couldn't afford to give up any ground. I was determined to meet this beast head-on and Bart was coming with me.

We had discussed establishing a routine for him. We were going back to the basics. Bart was in agreement with all of this, but the reality of the situation was I was taking charge of his health. He was turning to me for help, and I was going to help him help himself. Bart's self-esteem was shattered. I felt that Bart needed to see as much success as possible. If I did everything for him, I was convinced that he would become dependent upon me. Bart had already begun to be needy. I didn't sit back and crack a whip. Everything that Bart did the following day we did together or he did it himself. I made him breakfast and directed him each step of the way, but Bart took the steps. They seem so small now, and they are things that we all take for granted, but for Bart, on this Wednesday in March 2006, they were huge.

The Next Morning

Our day began at 6 a.m. with Bart and me in our new roles. I was now caregiver and Bart was the patient. I woke Bart and told him to get in the shower. I would like for you to take notice of the fact that I "told" Bart. This was not typical of our relationship. Bart and I have always had great respect for each other, but I have never had this role before. I also want to make note that the direction that I gave Bart was not at all demeaning. I was loving, positive, and most importantly I was firm.

After the day before, this was one of Bart's most difficult times. The mornings would continue to be challenging for quite some time. This is when more of his emotions began to emerge. Bart seemed to be weakest in all respects upon arising. He would often cry and his movements were so slow. I would tell him what he needed to do immediately and what he would be doing next. Often I would need to tell him more than once. For example, I would tell him to get in the shower, get dressed, and come to the table for his breakfast. I would have his clothes laid out for him and his breakfast prepared. He would look at me with the same blank expression and sometimes nod his head. He would plead with me to go back to bed and complain that he hurt so badly. I never allowed him to go back to bed. Again, this was my fear of regression. I did, however, allow him several breaks and opportunities to rest.

When I woke Bart, he sat on the side of the bed and cried. This was so pitiful, and I was brokenhearted for him, but in my mind this was temporary. My focus remained on improving this situation. As bad as this was, I knew that Bart wanted to get through it. I say this because I knew how Bart was before he became plagued with depression and how he was as we discussed this course of treatment. He was very willing to pursue these options. He wanted to feel better and he trusted me. We were going to do whatever it took to move beyond this state of agony.

I hugged him, kissed him, told him that I loved him, and encouraged him. I would do this often. I would also provide him a limited amount of time with each activity. When he would tell me that he just needed to sit on the side of the bed for a minute, I would allow him. I would tell him that I only wanted him to sit there for a specific number of minutes. When the clock read the designated time, I wanted him to get up and go to the shower. I would also tell him that I did not want him getting back in bed. Bart was very compliant. When he was in the shower, I would prepare his breakfast, lay out his clothes, get his medicine (as prescribed after seeing an MD), and his Bible. I would always give him a warning a few minutes prior with everything that he did. So for his shower, I would go to the bathroom door and tell him that he needed to be finishing up, then go back a few minutes later and tell him that it was time to get out of the shower.

I realize that this may seem somewhat mundane, but I wanted to share the experiences of this day because never experiencing a breakdown personally, I was amazed at how encompassing a nervous breakdown can be. I also want to share the accomplishments that Bart made in one day. I do not want to be misleading. Bart had so far to go, and we were not anywhere close at this time. Life was going to be bad before it got better, but we began changing his life on this day. And for Bart, it was worth it.

When Bart came to the table that morning, I told him that I wanted him to eat what he could and read his Bible. He was told when he should have these tasks completed. Once again, I would signal him to begin wrapping up and then return in time to move to the next step of the day.

I offered explanation with each step of this day. Bart needed to establish a new routine. He needed help preparing and taking control of his day. I was concerned about helping him establish a healthy and balanced lifestyle—a healthy and balanced mind, body, and spirit. When Bart completed breakfast, he was told to go upstairs (this is where his surveying office was located), and begin with #1 on his list of things to do. He just nodded his head, accepting the instructions. I followed him upstairs and reviewed #1 with him. He slowly began. I told him that I was going downstairs, I would be back, and what I expected from him in that time frame. Once again, he simply nodded his head and said, "Ok" as tears welled up in his eyes and began to stream down his face. I hugged him and reassured him and promised him a break when I returned.

With Bart upstairs, I went down to care for our three small children. At the time, they were 6 years, 3 years, and 19 months old. After the kids' needs were met, I returned upstairs to Bart. He had completed the assigned task and was ready for a break. I agreed. We began to talk. I sat in his lap as he talked and cried. He was extremely emotional all day. He said that he just wanted to rest. He knew how I felt about him going back to bed, and he never has been a big recliner man. As a matter of fact, from the time we got married, he has always said that he didn't want to be one of those guys who spent his time in a recliner and he hasn't. He rarely even sits in his.

Bart said that he wanted to lie down on the floor so that he could rest. I relented. He stretched out on the floor on his stomach. He commented about how much relief this gave him from the physical discomfort that was so prominent. As with everything else that he did that day, this too was only for a time. Now I wanted him to be able to experience relief, so he was allowed breaks frequently throughout the day. These breaks were brief.

Following Bart's break, he was scheduled to complete another task on his list and then go for a walk. These tasks were no different than anything else on this day. They were slow. My thoughts for Bart's walk were to incorporate exercise into his lifestyle and routine. I realized at this time that any physical activity for him was not going to be intense, and I simply wanted him to begin the habit and get some fresh air. When he completed his walk, he returned upstairs for another break. After he was guided to the next task on the list, I prepared lunch for him and our children.

Our next item that demanded attention was a customer communication issue. Over time, Bart's communication with his customers had begun to diminish. This was something that struck me with such surprise because Bart has always exercised strong communication skills with me. As a matter of fact, communication has always been one of the strengths of our relationship. He has always been very clear and forthright with his needs and feelings, as well as a wonderful listener. With that being said, this was yet another eye-opening experience for me. What I began to witness was that Bart wasn't communicating at all. I was aware that he had been having some difficulty for some time. When he would talk to me about situations, I would provide my input and often times I was surprised at how he was leaving conversations. One reason for my surprise was because of what I have just mentioned, but also because I don't communicate that way with anyone. I am very clear in my positions, and I don't like leaving things vague. I don't operate with a "read my mind" attitude and I don't like being treated that way by anyone. So it seemed so unnatural to see Bart communicating this way. He wouldn't even attempt to defend himself or his actions. He wasn't exerting any effort to prevent confusion. This in turn was causing him difficulty with his work and his customers.

Bart was his own worst enemy. All he had to do was offer some explanation to his customers. He would never have appreciated someone dealing with him in this way. He was doing quality work, but there are times when his work requires some explanation for the customer. Otherwise, the wrong conclusion is left for the customer. A customer's interpretation tends to minimize the amount and necessity of all the work that is involved in completing a survey.

With that being said, the next task of the day for Bart was to forge ahead with some work toward better customer communication relations. He currently had a project that he was working on that involved the local city planning commission. When the planning commission is involved, Bart becomes the liaison between the customer and the planning commission. The planning commission dictates the requirements of the customer. These requirements don't come all at once, and Bart has no control over any of these matters. The customer is not aware of this because this is oftentimes their only experience with circumstances of this kind, and since Bart is oftentimes the bearer of "bad news," he is also the one that receives the brunt of customer frustration. This is where I was seeing a significant breakdown in Bart's communication. He wasn't providing extra insight into the situation. From the customer's perspective, it appeared that Bart was not doing his job. When the customer would express frustration, Bart was not explaining that it was not his doing, but the city. He would in turn become frustrated with the customer. Obviously, this was not a healthy working relationship and not one that Bart would have been pleased with had he been a customer. I am not faulting Bart. There are issues about these situations that are beyond Bart's control. I did, however, feel that he could have improved in areas where he did have control such as anticipating possible problems and keeping the customer informed. Bart has since made several changes in his business to improve so much along with customer relations.

Life leading up to the breakdown had continued to become increasingly foggy for Bart. Goals had been forgotten or maybe the path to them was unclear. Nevertheless, survival was the primary focus. When any of us allow ourselves to take our eyes off the prize, it becomes too easy to get caught up in the predicament.

I say that to make this point. As I write about this particular work situation, I realize some questions may come to mind. *Why won't Bart defend himself? Why is he taking the blame here when he could offer an explanation that would eliminate at least some of the confusion?* It seems that this would be an opportunity for Bart to foster a positive relationship with his client. I found myself asking Bart these questions on several occasions. The answer was depression. Remember, this situation that I am sharing was during the breakdown. The nervous breakdown had been coming on for a long time, so Bart's behavior had also been moving this way for a long time. Due to this survival mode, Bart had become reactive rather than proactive, and it took some time for him to be able to see the difference. It was truly a forest for the trees situation.

The rest of the afternoon was consumed with resolving this issue. Fortunately, we had some help with the communication between Bart and this customer. Our preacher and his wife, Bruce and Rachel Reeves, are very close friends of ours and also knew the client much better than we did. Bart had called Bruce the night before to talk about his mental state. They came by and were surprised and concerned about Bart's condition. So when the client called Bruce, he and Rachel called me. We were all working together to keep peace, protect Bart in this fragile state, and provide the client with all that he was entitled to by improving the communication. This could not have been done without the help of Bruce and Rachel, and as you will see throughout this bout with depression, help was imperative to persevere.

By the end of this workday, Bart had accomplished so much. I was and still am so very proud of him. The effort that he put forth that day was phenomenal. It came from somewhere deep inside him. Yes, I did everything I knew to do to keep him from giving up, but Bart has that "don't quit" attitude that is a part of his existence. It was there then and it is there now. That was the part of him to which I was earnestly seeking to appeal.

After Bart finished the workday, we took a break on the deck and discussed the events of the day. Bart was able to see all that he had accomplished. He was proud, but still void of basically any emotion other than sadness. This was a Wednesday and we go to church on Wednesday night. I asked Bart if he felt like going. My concern was always his dignity. His emotional state was extremely fragile, and I didn't want him to be in a situation that was beyond his ability. Honestly, I was comfortable with the idea of him staying home. He was physically, mentally, and emotionally drained. He said that he wanted to go. This surprised me but I didn't discourage him. If he felt that he could handle it, I would do whatever I needed to do to allow him the opportunity.

I phoned my mother-in-law that evening to tell her of Bart's achievements of the day. First of all, this is a woman who is a mother through and through. Bart is her only son, but it wouldn't matter if he was one of ten, she would still adore him. She loves like a mom. She was here the day before and knew Bart's state. Patsy also knew that something had not been right about Bart for some time. She had asked me on several occasions about him. I knew that he was handling an amazing amount of stress, but I also knew that nothing could be done until he truly allowed it. I didn't see it coming the way she did. I don't know if she expected a nervous breakdown, but I know that she anticipated something. A momma knows.

My mother-in-law, Patsy, and myself.

When she answered the phone, I told her that I wanted her to know that she could be proud of her son. She began to cry. There has never been a doubt that Patsy is and has always been proud of her son. Anyone who knows her knows it. But today was different and we both knew it. I told her about his day. I knew that she was very concerned and would be extremely relieved to know of his progress. I also knew that it couldn't ever be easy for a mother to "sit on the sidelines" while her son was in distress. She did because she trusted me, but that doesn't mean it was easy. Before our conversation was over, I told her that I would keep her informed and she was so appreciative.

Our day ended with Bart and me making a list of things to do for the following day. This was by far the beginning of many challenging days that were to come.

Chapter 3
MY BIRTHDAY

My birthday was on a Sunday two months after Bart's breakdown. Bart had been given medicine (Lorazepam 1mg) on the Friday before at the Emergency Room. He slept most of Saturday. He would stay in our guest bedroom (the purple room) and lock the door. I would check on him periodically, and he would say that he had been praying, even though he would look as though he had been asleep. I knew that I was fast approaching my breaking point. As much as I loved Bart, he was killing me.

I had been shouldering him and this condition while trying to care for our children, straighten out our financial situation, and maintain as much of a normal lifestyle as possible. When he was given this medicine and was sleeping so much, I knew that I couldn't go in that direction. This Friday that I have mentioned was one of the days of his panic attacks, and he called his father, and his father took him to the hospital.

Prior to the panic attack and call to his father, Bart and I had spoken on the phone. I had found a huge hole in the side of the bathtub in the guest bathroom. I called him and asked him about it. He said that he didn't know anything about it. He is the one who uses this bathroom regularly because it is on the other side of the house, and he likes his privacy. I was aggravated about it. We didn't have an argument, but he knew that I was unhappy about finding this and having no explanation. This led him into the panic attack. Late Saturday afternoon I needed to run an errand. I made him go with the children and me because I was scared to leave him alone. I was confident that he would sleep, but I didn't want to take a chance. When we got home, I told him that I was at my breaking point. I wasn't yelling at him. I was very calm before I began sobbing. I told him that I couldn't go in this direction with this condition. It seemed as if we were taking a wrong turn that was causing him to regress. I needed a break (only from this type of care). I urged him to go to his parents and stay. He could come and go as he liked, and he would be home a lot as well, because his office was here. I needed some help, and I was going to talk to someone. He began to cry and said that he didn't want to leave. I reminded him that he was going to his parents anyway every time there was an issue to face. I seemed to be triggering his panic attacks and that wasn't helping either of us. I told him I knew that he would be fine at his parents' house. I would never suggest that he go anywhere that he wouldn't be given the utmost care.

Bart went back to sleep. I called my father-in-law to make arrangements for him to stay with Bart if he didn't go to church with us the following morning. During this conversation, he told me to hide the medicine that Bart had received from his ER visit. He said that it was powerful and highly addictive. I did.

Sunday morning (my birthday) – The children and I got ready for church. Bart had slept in the guest room the night before and didn't get up until we were on our way out. I had called my father-in-law and told him to come over. He and my mother-in-law arrived promptly. Before they got there and as the children were loading in the Suburban, I went upstairs to tell Bart the plans. He had gone upstairs to his office upon arising.

He was lying on his stomach on the floor. (This is something that he did often during the intense time of his breakdown.) He raised his head and looked at me. He wished me happy birthday. I thanked him and told him that we were leaving for church and that his parents were on their way. I also told him what work he needed to do. (I had had to do this—manage his workload—since the crash.) He shook his head in agreement with the saddest expression on his face.

As I walked out the door, his parents pulled up. I told them where he was, that the medicine was hidden, and to make sure that he followed the work schedule. They wished me Happy Birthday and said that they would do as I requested.

When we got to church, I had begun to cry. I was doing my best to hold my composure, but it wasn't working. I took the children to class, and as I turned around from leaving Allie's classroom, Rachel was there and asked me how I was doing. I started crying again. I told her that this was killing me. We talked briefly and she asked me if I needed to go home. I said no. I knew that Bart was ok. I realize that I am using "ok" loosely. Actually, he was simply out of danger. At that point, while I was so distraught I was also a bit relieved because I was getting a break. His behavior was so unpredictable and out of character for him when he was alone; however, when he was with supervision, he was rather predictable because he was very accommodating to the direction given by the supervision.

Rachel and I walked back to Bruce's office and stayed in there. We talked and I cried. When class was over, she sent Bruce in and took care of my children. Bruce came in and talked briefly. He assured me that he would get in touch with a therapist for me.

When we got home, Bart met us at the Suburban door, picked me up off the ground and hugged me. He had showered and dressed. (Once again—the emotional roller coaster.) That was the Bart that I had known. I would see glimpses of him—the real Bart from time to time. This was one of those times. We went in the house and I opened some gifts. My in-laws took the children for the afternoon. Bart and I went to eat and came back to the house to finish some of his work. That afternoon was one of those brief escapes back to a time where it was just Bart and me and no depression. I was willing to take what I could get.

You know I think those brief glimpses of what had always been and what I so desperately hoped would be again gave me "whatever" to keep going. It gave me a hope that Bart was still in there somewhere. He wanted to come back, and it reaffirmed my fierce determination that I wasn't giving up. In my heart, I always knew there was something worth fighting for.

Chapter 4
LIFE UNFOLDING

When Bart crashed, he was two months behind on everything. I discovered this piece by piece. It wasn't like Bart just said here's the problem. I am depressed and suffering from a nervous breakdown. We are two months behind on everything. Our finances are disastrous and I am doing my best to correct it, but I need you to take over. If only it had been that simple. This conclusion came over time and so often by surprise. This problem had so many layers and that is how it presented itself—in layers. Every time I felt that I was in a position to wrap my arms around this situation, another facet would unfold. This was so difficult because this information wasn't coming from Bart. It was coming from everywhere but Bart. When I would confront Bart with the information, he would have a panic attack.

Of course, hind sight is 20/20, but this is one time that had I known ahead of time that Bart was suffering as he was, determined to improve the circumstances without the necessary tools, then it would have been much easier to be sympathetic toward his needs. As a result, he came across as dishonest. The current behavior was so unlike him in the past. The strongest attribute in Bart's favor, regardless of what was happening, was his past behavior and the sincerity of his actions. I could not forget this and it was making life so confusing.

I remember being in our kitchen and looking at Bart. We had been discussing something related to his health, work, or finances. We weren't arguing, but I remember that it was something that was emotional and painful for me, yet I couldn't allow myself to cry because this would bring about more pain for him. Every time that I expressed sadness this would result in Bart becoming even sadder. Everything was sad and painful for him at this time, and he was trying so hard to stay above sadness. When I expressed it, he would feel guilty and sad, because now I was feeling this way. It was an emotional nightmare. But in the middle of all of this, I remember noticing how pitiful he looked and how hurt I was. It was at that moment that I thought, if the roles had been reversed, I would not have been able to shake him loose from me even if I tried. If I was the one struggling as he was, there is no way in this world that he would ever leave me or not try to do all that he could to help me. Neither one of us took our vows lightly when we made them, but it is the reassurance that Bart has always provided that allowed me to see and believe it even more when it seemed that we were on opposing teams.

As life and circumstances were unfolding, I had begun actively battling everything coming our way. I was in constant contact with the bank. By this time, Bart was not allowed at the bank or the mailbox because it brought on added anxiety and too strong a temptation to fall back into the old behaviors. This was strictly enforced. The girls at the bank knew it. They were to notify me immediately if Bart tried to do any banking of any kind. You see, Bart's recovery was a group effort, and I was reaching out wherever it was necessary. The girls at the bank were working with me on a daily basis to get this thing turned around. There were several days following the breakdown that I would take a check that Bart would collect and go straight to the bank in order to beat checks that would be hitting our account. I learned all of the cut-off times and lived within those parameters. As a matter of fact, there were several times that the girls would be guessing times on the exact minute that I would make it in the door. One time I was there waiting on Bart to make it back in town with a check so that I would be the one to make the deposit. I met him in the parking lot of the bank. During this time, that was the closest that he got to the bank.

Credit cards were also off limits for him. He could not recall payments that he had authorized, and it was better if he was completely removed from this part of our lives for the time being. It is because of this that the following situation escalated as it did.

We received a letter from one of the credit cards about a phone authorized payment that I hadn't made. It was a Wednesday, so I called the company when we got home from church. The situation was resolved. I had asked Bart if he had authorized the transaction. He said that he hadn't, and then he said he couldn't remember. I told him that I wanted every credit card in his possession. This led to an argument, but he brought me some credit cards.

The next morning an argument broke out about honesty. Bart stormed out of the bedroom. I got in the shower. When I got out and finished getting ready, I went to the kitchen. I began looking around for him. I couldn't find him anywhere. All of the vehicles were home. I began to get nervous. He had never tried to hurt himself, but I was scared that maybe he could have done something now. I knew if he had, that I had to find him before our children did. I had to prevent our children from walking up on something that could leave them forever scarred.

I began looking in the bathtubs and closets. I walked around the fence. I would

keep an eye on our dogs because after I didn't find him, I just knew that he had to have gone somewhere on foot. I felt sure that if he was anywhere near the fence, the dogs would indicate it. As the time passed, my fear and anger grew.
I called my father-in-law and asked him to come over. I had originally planned to take the girls to him so that he could watch them while I took our son to get his physical for Kindergarten. Due to the current circumstances, I needed him to come to our house instead. Bruce Reeves called, which struck me as odd because he never called that early in the morning. When I answered the phone, Bruce asked me how things were going. I told him not too good. I had no idea where Bart was. He said, "You don't know where he is?" I said, "I have no idea." He said, "He's at Dickey and Patsy's." Patsy had just called Bruce and asked him to come and talk with Bart. Bruce said that he would be back in town later in the morning and would be there. I asked Bruce how he got there and Bruce said, "I guess Patsy came and got him."

At this point, I was livid. From my point of view, this man had lied to me the night before and authorized credit card transactions after he had agreed to leave it alone. I had to insist that he give up all of the credit cards in his possession and that was followed by an argument. By the following morning, in his mind, every-thing should be just fine. Eight hours of sleep compared to, for all I knew at this point, eight years of dishonesty should be equivalent. When I was quiet the next morning, the discussion of dishonesty and trust began and ended at an argument and him storming out of the bedroom. Based on what our lives had become and how unpredictable and irrational his behavior was, anything was possible. His health had been very fragile, and even though he hadn't attempted suicide, he had made comments about how much easier it would be if he could just "go away."

Most of all, I was hurt. Regardless of how much help I had given Bart, it felt as if he was intentionally turning away from me. We would take one step forward and then so many back. He had the luxury of walking out if he got mad. I had to stay and face it. We have children and responsibilities. This all fell on my shoulders while Bart was in this compromised state. He had brought my greatest fears to the forefront of my mind. I was scared to death that losing him was becoming a reality. I have always lived with this fear in a rational way. I don't think that it is uncommon. It is a fear of something happening to Bart and our children wouldn't have their dad, I wouldn't have my husband, and I would be left to raise them alone. It is a fear of living my life without my best friend.

Throughout Bart's suffering and recovery, I could always see improvement. It wasn't fast and there were plenty of set-backs, but there was always progression. This was without a doubt one of the set-backs, and it wasn't going to turn around over night.

My father-in-law made it to our house as I was getting off the phone with Bruce. Dickey knew when he came in how I felt. I filled him in briefly. He stayed with the girls while I took Todd to the doctor. While I was at the doctor, I talked with him about Bart's behavior. Our doctor didn't have a lot of answers, but one revelation that he shared was that depression doesn't cause a person to be unable to determine right from wrong. This would prove to be very valuable information that would present itself on various occasions as time passed.

My father-in-law, Allie, and Bart.

Bart spent a big part of the day at his parents' house. Bruce went by and visited with him and then Bart's parents took him to visit with a counselor. In the meantime, Bruce came by the house and visited with me. He said that Bart was proud that Bruce would be talking to me. He claimed that he didn't realize that he never told me that he was leaving. He didn't realize what he had put me through.

Bruce and I talked for quite awhile. He helped provide some focus and support. After Bruce left, Dickey called. He had Bart and Patsy with him, and they were on their way to our house. I told Dickey that I didn't want Bart here. I asked him if Bart was with him. He told me that he was. I again said that I didn't want him here, but that I would listen to him (Dickey).

When they got to our house, the children and I were in the backyard. Patsy came out there. Bart stuck his head out the door and asked me to come in. I said that I would, but I called Dickey, who was coming through the gate, to come with me. One of the reasons for this was because Bart was claiming that I would get mad and not listen to him. I would get mad because I would receive information from all over the place that should have come from him and most often was contradicting what he was saying. I would get frustrated, and Bart would get anxious and experience a panic attack every time issues came up that he didn't want to discuss. When information was coming to my knowledge he would get nervous. He would often claim that he didn't want anything to change between us, yet it seemed that everything that he was doing was to ensure that this in fact would happen. I wanted a witness.

The three of us sat down in the living room. I sat in a recliner facing Bart on the sofa. Dickey sat in the other recliner. Bart began. He apologized for what had happened earlier that morning. He claimed that he didn't realize what he had put me through earlier that day. He shared some of what the counselor had discussed with him. I listened and then I had my say.

I made it clear that I understood that Bart was suffering with depression, and it was real. I also made it clear that the rest of us were also being affected. One thing that was so frustrating about Bart's situation was how he would attempt to justify everything. I shared the conversation that I had with our doctor and emphasized the fact that someone suffering with depression still knows right from wrong. This point led into the events of the morning. Bart claimed that he didn't know that I didn't know where he was until later in the day.

Before today, Bart had several days where he would have such difficulty getting his day started or he would have issues that would prevent him from completing his work. In this conversation, I expressed the importance of Bart doing his part, which involved surveying. That was all. He was expected to get up, survey and collect. His parents and I were doing everything else. All that he should be focusing on was his job, and with that being said, any and all of the breaks for lengthy conversations during daylight hours were forbidden. If he needed to talk, it better be when it was dark. He nodded his head in agreement.

Bart would tell me that he was going to do better and offer what seemed to be empty promises. I remember telling him to stop and not to tell me that anymore. Just focus on doing it. If he did it, I would see it. I asked him what his plans were for the rest of the day. He said that he was coming home. I said that I didn't think so. I told him that we had this conversation on Saturday (the day before my birthday on Sunday) about him staying with his parents and that I was at my limit. He was killing me. I also told him that I deserved better than that. I wouldn't allow him or anyone else to treat me the way he had today. I don't treat him with such disregard, and I do not intend to allow it for myself or our children. It seemed that every time that he felt any pressure, he would look for an escape and it was via his parents. The positive part of Bart turning to his parents was that the three of us were working together, and when he was turning to them, he was safe. The down side of this was that regardless of where he was turning, it was away from me. They were doing their best to help in any way that they could, but inevitably it was necessary that he face the fire. Since this was a place of peace for him, I suggested that he stay there for a while. I was definite about him staying this night. He began to cry and wanted to know if he could come home. I said that he needed to get his things for work tomorrow and be in the field at daylight and not to come in until dark. He would be able to see the children, but he needed to be focusing on his work and his health. Bart accepted the terms with reservation.

We were outside as Bart and his parents were leaving. He hugged the kids. They didn't understand the situation nor did they know that he wasn't staying at home that night. They just knew that he was leaving and were secure that he would be back. They were resilient throughout and seemed to possess a keen awareness. Bart looked at me with tears in his eyes, and I told him that he would be fine. He nodded and turned to leave.

Cash McMillen, our cousin, pulled up as they were leaving. He got out of his truck and asked me what was going on. He had been by earlier when Bruce was here and then he saw Bart leaving. I didn't really answer him. He pressed the issue a bit, and so I asked him if we could keep this between us. He said yes, so I began. I remember telling him that Bart was lying to me. I told him about the events of the past 24 hours. We went out on the deck and talked for quite awhile. He shared behaviors of Bart that he had witnessed in order to help make sense of this mystery. Cash has worked with Bart for at least ten years, and he has a good head on his shoulders, so I value what he has to say. Before Cash left, Bruce called to check on the situation. I updated him. He asked if I was ok. I told him that I was and that Cash was here. We had been talking. Cash offered to take the children for awhile or help however he could. I thanked him, but told him that I really needed them right now. I planned to take them to Burger King and let them play. I wanted to mix up our schedule so that it wouldn't be noticeable to them that Bart wasn't at home. I didn't know if I could answer any questions about his whereabouts without losing my composure.

I have to say, this was a night that I needed. Don't get me wrong, I always want Bart home, but the Bart that I had been dealing with was not the same. I was receiving a small break from the constant pressure. I knew that Bart was taken care of at his parents' house. He was safe. On this one night, I knew I didn't have to be on guard.

I woke up the following morning very anxious. I was nervous that Bart would come in that morning and seeing him home at that time would mean that everything that we went through the day before would have been for nothing. I remember beginning to panic. My heart was racing and my breathing was shallow. For whatever reason, I turned on a CD of some of my favorite songs and tried to sing along. I was hoping to force myself to breathe normally and calm down. It worked. I had to stay mentally composed regardless of what it took. My family depended on it.

When Bart didn't come by, I was relieved and sad, but I forced myself to stay focused. I occupied my mind with prayer. 1 Thessalonians 5:17 tells us to pray without ceasing. This is what I did. So many times throughout 2006 I felt that even though we had some very special people around that contributed so much, to my Heavenly Father was the only place that I wanted to turn. I was convinced that ONLY with God would we make it through. He had the answers and I needed to know them.

The children and I followed our routine. I talked with my father-in-law who told me that Bart had rolled out early that morning as he had agreed. He told me about Bart's night. Dickey said that he would come out later that afternoon. I was so relieved to hear how Bart had started his day.

When my father-in-law got to our house that afternoon, he updated me on Bart's state. He said that Bart was really humble and that I could get Bart to do about anything right now. He asked me if I was going to let Bart come home that night. He said that he supported me and my decision. I had prayed all day about it, and I told him that if Bart would do the following, then he could come home. It was up to him.

1. Sincerely apologize
2. Acknowledge what he had been doing was wrong instead of justifying his actions
3. Change his behavior (which I realized would not be immediate, but better start turning that way)

I told my father-in-law that he could pass that along if he so chose. He called me shortly after he left and said that he had talked to Bart and that Bart had been joking and laughing. Dickey's intentions were sincere. He felt that this would be something that would make me feel better, but it crushed me. I was heartbroken that Bart could be in the state that he was the day before, treat me with such disregard, and be so happy today. It hit me so hard. It seemed that I was the one making Bart so miserable. I was in tears. I called Bruce and told him about the phone conversation with Dickey. He said, "What?" He was as surprised as I was since he had been involved with both of us so much the day before. He asked me if anyone was with Bart. I told him that Cash and Matt Finley were with him. (I would trust these guys with my life.) He said he wanted to call Cash and that he would call me back. When Bruce called, he told me that Cash said that Bart had worked all day, but it had been hard for him. He said that Cash and Matt were doing their best to lighten Bart's mood. Bart hadn't been laughing all day long. I was not proud to hear that Bart was struggling, but I was proud to see consistency and that I wasn't the one making Bart miserable.

Later that evening, Bart called. He said that he worked hard that day. He told me that he did what I said to do—he had been in the field at daylight and worked until dark. He said that it wasn't easy, but that he didn't quit. Bart asked me if he could come home. I told him that I was proud of how he had worked that day, and that he could come over, but I didn't think that he needed to stay. He asked if he could talk to me. I said yes.

I remember experiencing so many emotions simultaneously. This happened throughout the entire "overcoming the breakdown" period. But the time between this particular phone call and Bart's arrival was one of the most significant. I remember feeling so excited that he had called and that he was coming over. This was how I was when we were dating. I was always ready to see him. The other emotions were nervous, anxiety, relief, and determination. I was nervous and anxious because of all that had happened. I was relieved that he had worked as we had agreed he would. He was coming over, and I had determined since we had come this far, that I was standing my ground. My stipulations were for our individual well-being, as well as the health of our relationship.

When Bart walked through the door, I almost cried. (I was still Bart's emotional barometer at this point.) I didn't say a word. I just listened. Bart sincerely apologized, acknowledged the mistakes minus justification, and we talked for a long time. I will admit, I was so mad at him the day before, but after he came by that night, I really wanted him to stay. He stayed.

This was one of the most significant turning points. Bart finally opened up and shared his fears of this situation. Basically, he was afraid that if I knew about the state of our finances, that I would think less of him and possibly not want to be with him anymore. He admitted that I had never given him any reason to believe this, but that he never wanted to disappoint me. This was the first time throughout all of the problems that Bart actually shared his perspective. This helped so much because I really wanted to like Bart again. I never stopped loving him, but liking him was often becoming debatable. I believed Bart.

Sheree and Bart

Chapter 5
BOYCE

We finally reached a point where the facts seemed to indicate that Bart was having his trouble because it was embarrassing for him, and he didn't want me to feel differently about him. He had said as much when we had had a long talk following the night that he spent at his parents' house. I was afraid to accept this without professional validation because if I was wrong, Bart's recovery could stall. I desperately wanted to believe this, but I was aware that I could want this conclusion for the wrong reason. Our lives were in upheaval. We both wanted peace. I was physically, mentally, and emotionally drained, not to mention the agony that Bart was enduring. Bart had been guilty of "quick fixes" for some time now. When he felt pressure, he would do what he had to in order to delay the inevitable. Obviously, the closer that his breakdown came, the more frequently he made "quick fixes." This had become such a force of survival that Bart couldn't allow himself the opportunity to do anything but operate in this manner. He was building a house of cards.

One of my many mantras had become "deal with the facts, the facts don't lie." So many times I had faulted Bart for making decisions based on emotion. I refused to be a hypocrite. We were in this too deep, and the only way to find our way out was to see it through. I was convinced that if we strayed from this course, everything that we had experienced thus far was for naught, and there would still be questions not answered and problems not solved. I was spent but I wasn't quitting. There was way too much at stake. Bart and I had discussed a specific analogy relating to this situation. (I love analogies.) The analogy was an open wound. If a wound is patched on the surface without cleansing it of the infection that lies underneath, the problems that loom are inevitably going to be much larger than before. Perseverance was the only path away from this pain.

I needed someone (a professional) to validate this and Boyce, in fact, did validate it. Boyce Barger is a Christian counselor with whom our friends, Bruce and Rachel, put me in contact. Bart had met with a counselor at a counseling agency in our area. I had actually been with him on a few of his sessions, and I was comfortable with the counselors, but I wanted to go to a different place, a different counselor. Bart had his problems and I had mine. We were handling depression from two entirely different perspectives. We were both trying to survive depression and all that our roles entailed.

I was able to meet with Boyce on a Sunday afternoon in mid May 2006. I was ready. I had so many of my own issues that had developed as well as the need for validation for the conclusions that I felt that I had reached. Bart was very supportive and encouraging of the session. He is always supportive of anything that I want to do or feel that I need. Bart was well enough to care for the kids while I was away, and Rachel went with me for support.

The session was more than worthwhile. Boyce came highly recommended and didn't disappoint. It was so enjoyable to speak with someone who could help me meet my needs and frame my emotions. We had very dear friends and family around us during this time, and their contribution was immeasurable, but I needed someone trained in these matters to make sense of the situation.

During the session, I shared as much as possible about Bart, me, and our lives prior and present. One of Boyce's comments was that I definitely seemed to have looked at Bart and the situation from all angles. He concluded that I was in fact the most important person to Bart, and Bart didn't want to disappoint me. I was so relieved following the session. I felt such a peace after expressing my thoughts and feelings. I wasn't under the delusion that our problems were magically solved. I was, however, convinced that Bart was a good guy suffering from depression and that I had legitimate hurts, fears, and concerns. This bout of depression wasn't affecting only Bart. This visit allowed me to put this situation in perspective and provided a new strength with which to endure.

When I came home, Bart met me at the door and asked how it went, but that I shouldn't feel obligated to tell him anything. I shared everything with Bart. He began to cry and said that what Boyce had said was the truth. I was relieved because I really wanted to believe Bart, but I was afraid that if I did without some sort of validation, I might be functioning based on emotion and not facts. And I knew that if it were just emotion, I wouldn't be helping either of us. I knew from the beginning of the breakdown that until we reached the heart of the matter, Bart would never be able to truly heal. I also knew that this situation was highly emotional. It was imperative that we stick to the facts and face them.

This was undoubtedly a huge turning point in the road to recovery.

Chapter 6
LEARNING ABOUT DEPRESSION

Since Bart's recovery from his breakdown, I have learned so much and gained an enormous amount of sympathy, respect, appreciation, and admiration for him and what he endured. I have found myself at times experiencing the role that Bart held for so long, and I tell you, **I do not know how he made it as long as he did**. He is an incredibly strong person. It is certainly not something that I could do.

There is no way that I could wrap my mind around his condition at the time because I had never experienced something like this. I have been depressed. I have hurt. I have never had an experience like this. All I knew was that I wanted him to get better, and I wanted to help him help himself. I didn't want him to be dependent upon me, anyone, or anything else. We all need others in our lives, and we need to be needed, but there is a difference between needing fulfilling relationships in our lives and being dependent upon someone or something to survive.

With this evolving depression, so many emotions surfaced for me. I have never been so mad at Bart. There was so much confusion surrounding his breakdown. As this problem unfolded, I began to get hurt. I seemed to be the target for all of Bart's misguided decisions. Initially, I was definitely concerned about Bart's health and condition, but I wasn't truly aware of the full magnitude of his problem. I knew that finances and his job were causing him extreme stress. What I didn't know was the severity of our state of affairs. When Bart crashed, we were two months behind on all of our bills. His books for his business were a mess and customer relations were more than frustrating. He had obviously become despondent with his work. Bart had been juggling bills for so long. He had customers that wouldn't pay and bills that had to be paid.

It took some time and lots of prayer for me to move beyond anger and blame. I blamed Bart for the problems that were there. I blamed him for keeping things from me. I blamed him for jeopardizing our relationship. I blamed him for decisions that he had made in business. As you can see, I have had growing to do myself.

I had so much frustration when I found myself shifting from my focus. My focus was Bart's health—mentally, physically, and emotionally. And this is where I had to stay. I could not allow even the slightest diversion in my path. I found that when I did, Bart and I both lost ground.

I know that it seems that I remained in a state of anger in 2006. That is quite the contrary. I share all of this to make this point. It is because of my feelings for Bart and my own dignity that I did get angry. It is through constant prayer and God given wisdom that I was able to set aside this anger and any other distractions to stay focused on Bart's improvement. His health was the most important. It was my choice and desire as he was showing improvement to work through my own anger and blame in order to grow and to learn what I could from all of this. This brings me to a realization that came to light. Under these circumstances, the motivation behind the appearance of dishonesty was the most important and where I had to keep my focus. I don't condone dishonesty, but there is a difference between lying to deceive and failing to provide information with the intent to improve. What I didn't realize at this time was that Bart really couldn't remember. Depression affects the ability to recall. It is the symptom of "foggy head." Something else that I didn't understand until much later was why, when he would answer me with "I'll take care of it," it was not a lie. I had to experience this for myself. Bart was always chasing the idea that he was about to turn things around. He did realize prior to his breakdown that this lifestyle had run its course, and everything was about to be exposed. This, along with his fear of what I would think of him when everything was exposed, resulted in his nervous breakdown.

Well as life has moved on, I have found myself in situations which bring Bart to the forefront of my mind. I realize now that when Bart would say, "I'll take care of it," he was doing his best under the circumstances. Bart would make commitments to pay bills based on money that he was promised to receive promptly, and then that money would take anywhere from days to weeks to get to him. This in turn would make him late on payments which would have so many effects. Now this is not that Bart didn't want to pay the bills or that he wasn't trying. He was trying so much so that it drove him to a nervous breakdown.

One piece of advice that came our way was to simply "cut expenses." I am in agreement with living inside your means, but this wasn't a situation where that was the case. Bart's business had been set up originally with big payments for extra equipment and hired help which left him with limitations on what could be cut. What he had left to cut were the essentials which he could not function without—electricity, phone, gas, etc. As for our personal expenses, we were not spending out of control, and they were not what were putting strain on his business, and it would be preposterous to imply such a thought. That would be like the tail wagging the dog. His business was to provide for his business and be a means of providing for his family. Cutting expenses was not the answer. When you get behind, it becomes a monster all its own and near impossible to overcome.

As frustrating as it has been with advice such as this, I have to refrain from acting on the frustration, but rather redirect it. One way that I do this is by taking a step back and realizing that this advice is shared because it is what they know and all they know. The intentions are sincere and with this I identify. I have been guilty myself of the same behavior. I have shared with you how I worked with Bart following his breakdown and how I relied on what I knew. My intentions were also sincere, but not always the most appropriate. They were, however, what I knew. So I share this instance because it allowed me to understand Bart's situation a bit better and reaffirmed the fact that you never truly know a person's situation until you stand in his shoes and look through his eyes.

I was guilty myself of faulting Bart of out-of-control spending because that was the appearance that was taking shape. Of course, this was not at all the only life altering bit of information coming my way at this time. I had to swallow a lot so to speak, and honestly, even then, this did not make sense based on Bart's character. But as I have said before, as his wife, I will be one who will be willing to pursue in order to see what is causing this picture to appear this way and accept the reality. It is so easy to pass judgment when you don't have all of the facts. It is so hard to pass judgment when you do.

Once again, it comes down to choices. So I choose not to focus on this as a point of distraction, but of motivation. It's my choice. This brings me to where I did place my focus.

When Bart's breakdown began, surviving immediately became the entire focus. It became one moment at a time, one step at a time. There was no plan for the future only maintaining an endurance of the present. When I think back to those darkest moments, I am still awestruck. Bart's condition was so fragile. Everything from his attitude to his zeal, or lack of, and everything in between was affected. He was slowly becoming someone so very different, so unrecognizable. His focus had done a 180 over time.

Very early on in Bart's recuperation we were in agreement that since he had hit rock bottom mentally, emotionally, and physically (financially was just around the corner), this was his opportunity to plant both feet on the ground for a firm foundation. At this point, he had nowhere to go but up. His focus began to change. We began working together to help him develop patterns and behaviors that would prevent the likelihood of a repeat breakdown or a prolonged depression.

Chapter 7
RELATIONSHIP

I want to share some insight about the relationship that Bart and I have. In order to have a more accurate view of the situations that took place in 2006, it will be helpful to know more about the two of us and how we function as a couple. Bart and I are very similar in some very important ways that provide many strengths to our marriage. We are both tenaciously loyal to the things that we hold dear. It just so happens that many of the things that we hold dear are the same: our faith, each other, and the relationship that we have, and our children. The list doesn't stop there, but those are the top. Everything that we do and the decisions that we make are in regard to continuously improving and securing those relationships. Please remember that we didn't wake up one day as loyal individuals or begin to have loyalty in our relationship sometime after one of our children was born. As individuals, loyalty is part of our character. We are that way, and we don't try to suppress that trait. It is who we are, and we make it a strength by making wise decisions that don't contradict who we are. Individually, we are loyal, and we brought that to our relationship and marriage. Giving up, getting out, or doing anything other than staying together forever is not even discussed, much less an option. We take that one step further with the respect that we have for each other. We each want the other to be completely happy.

If I had to prioritize the strengths of our relationship, communication would have to be at the top. This is not to say or imply that there aren't many others; however, this is the one that seems to top the list. Bart and I have always been able to communicate. When we were dating, we lived three hours apart. We spent most weekends together and spoke every night on the phone. We had large phone bills because we would talk for no less than an hour each night. We never viewed this as an expense. It was simply part of our relationship. Bart and I were and still are best friends.

Our relationship has always been easy, and what I mean by that is we both have always had a focus beyond the small stuff. For example, Bart has never been a neat freak, but by no means is he a slob. He is just not as neat as I would have things be. This is a decision that I made from the beginning. Call it compromise if you like, but I decided to be reasonable. I shared with him what really bothered

40

me and asked for his help. Problem solved. Bart was and always has been more than accommodating, and this is something that has worked both ways with us. We are always able to find common ground. (By the way, my neatness issues have continued to slide as children have come into our lives. I have my limits, but I have worked to keep this from overtaking me. When Bart says let's go do "whatever" and the kitchen is a mess, we go do "whatever." I am thrilled that he wants me to go, and the kitchen will be there when I get back. And you know, if we get back and it is clean, then lucky me.)

I have always had complete and total confidence in him. I would trust him beyond reason. Bart was always the spontaneous one. This has changed somewhat because we have a family, and our lifestyle doesn't allow for that right now. I am not spontaneous by nature. I need to do a little bit of planning and preparation. I loved Bart's spontaneous nature. It was exciting and fun. I never cared where we were going or what we would be doing. I have just always loved being with him.

Our dating experience was a magical time. We had so much fun. We both love being married, but for us marriage has been dating magnified. While our children are home, we intend to live that life to the fullest realizing all the while that this too is for a time, and when this time moves us to a new stage of life, we plan to find ourselves together. Bart and I have plans for our life when we are just the two of us again. This in no way means or implies that we are in a hurry to get there; however, we are realistic. We are raising our children to be independent, free-thinking individuals, guiding them as they find their passions and discover their talents. We expect to reach this goal, and part of attaining the goal is doing our part—letting go.

Bart and I had a wonderful dating experience. We met in college and became friends, although it wasn't until much later that we shared anything beyond friendship. When I think back on our dating experience, I have to smile. It was so much fun. We laughed so much, and I have to tell you, laughter is addictive. Bart is a funny guy with a fun sense of humor. Laughing is not at all foreign to him. He came along in my life when I really needed to laugh. I remember the first time Bart and I were together and laughing so hard. I was so surprised. He had tapped into an emotion that I had forgotten. We were and are forever buddies. I was crazy about him then, and I am crazy about him now.

The first time that I came to Conway with Bart was a weekend that was packed like a day in the movie "The Naked Gun." As a matter of fact, that is what we called it—our Naked Gun day. On Saturday, Bart had to take a test for school that lasted all morning. Afterwards, we visited his grandparents, went fishing, horseback riding, and watched the Tyson fight. You see—Naked Gun day. This is what dating Bart was like. Bart is always the plan man. He provides options for activities and restaurants. I am the one who makes the final decision because I am better at time management. My strength is not in the idea or plan part. We always had something to do. However, I want to emphasize the fact that we also had/ have as much fun piling up and watching our favorite sitcoms.

The point is we have always enjoyed each other, and that hasn't stopped. Of course, our lives have changed. We now have three small children. Anyone with children knows—**life changes**. We love it though. We have a few sayings in our home and one of them is—*We picked teams and we (Bart and I) are on the same team. It's us against them.* This may sound a bit silly, but it is an underlying strength of our relationship. We have always operated this way. It is a wonderful feeling to know that no matter what, you have someone on your team.

Bart and the kids having fun

One afternoon while we were dating, we had decided to go horseback riding. Bart's sister, JoEllen, went with us. JoEllen was on a horse that was old and clumsy which was funny and something that she took in stride. Bart's horse seemed to be behaving, but mine, on the other hand, was not. The three of us were riding on a dirt road with JoEllen in front and Bart and I were basically beside each other on horseback. As we were riding along, my horse turned his head and bit Bart's calf. Bart yelled and punched the horse. As I said, my horse was ornery so he was a bit difficult to predict. Luckily, the horse was as surprised as we were and didn't do anything but shake his head. I couldn't help it. I laughed and laughed. Bart punched the horse.

Bart's reactions have always been so funny to me. He is not extremely expressive or dramatic; he is, however, simple in his reactions and hilarious in his response. When something happens, I find myself watching him and anticipating his reaction.

Bart has always been a soft place to land. I know beyond a shadow of doubt that I am a better and stronger person with Bart. He is genuine. He has always been a good listener—too good sometimes. He remembers details, but when an issue is settled, it's over. This is something that I really appreciate. Bart discusses and fights fair.

With Bart being a father, I am able to see yet another side to him. He is a super dad. He is involved with each one of the kids and he truly wants to be. Every little girl wants that special relationship with their daddy, but not every little girl gets it. Our girls have it, and it is because Bart puts forth effort to know them and not simply co-exist. With our son, Bart has never held back. Todd knows that Bart loves him and is proud of him because Bart tells him so. Todd isn't left to gather this on his own. I am so proud to be experiencing parenthood with him.

Bart with Jenna and Todd

I wanted to share some significant stories about Bart and our relationship that would really provide you with how special Bart is. When those stories were read, it would be undeniable the changes that occurred in Bart during his depression. I don't have them. This is not at all because special events haven't happened. I just began to realize that to know Bart is to experience Bart, and our relationship isn't hinged on events. Our relationship is full of the little things that he does all of the time. Bigger things happen from time to time and they are special, but it is the day in, day out behav-

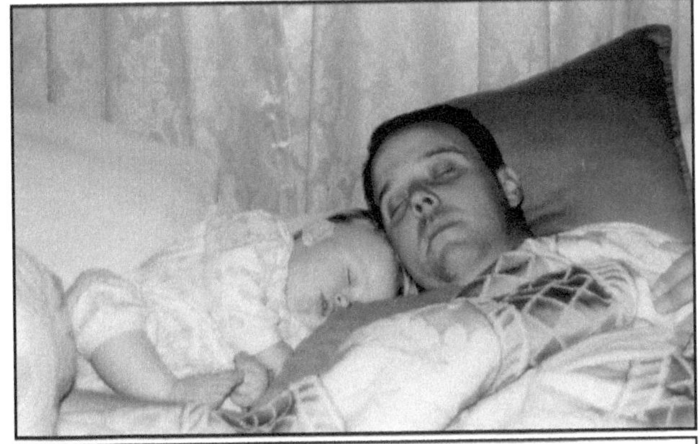

Todd and Bart

iors that provide the most accurate picture of Bart. He wants me to be happy, and he does things to make me feel special. It is not at all unusual for Bart to come home with a card, flowers, or both—just because. He is a devoted and involved husband who claims time to spend with me. Whenever I have expressed a need that I might have, Bart has immediately gone above and beyond to make sure that the need was met. He is my most favorite person and my very best friend. Bart is not perfect, not even close, and that is fine with me. He is, however, perfect for me. Bart loves me, completely and without reservation. He is true blue.

I believe that when you meet that someone, you know. This is how it happened with Bart and me. Bart was the one. I knew it and so did he. Now this wasn't something we shared in conversation initially. We just knew. When you meet that special someone, the question is not, could I live with this person? Rather, could I live without this person? My answer was no. I couldn't live my life without Bart, and as we live our lives, I am not me without him. He enhances my strengths and minimizes my weaknesses. We face life together. He is a large part of who I am. His health is my health; his sickness is my sickness. With that being said, when his depression began and his breakdown occurred, fighting through it was for us both. Our relationship was dependent upon his well being. Our health was dependent upon his well being. So even though at times it felt that I was carrying him, it was because our health and future were dependent upon it. Some may see my motivations as selfish, but they are far from selfish. My motivations are supported by my level of commitment to Bart, our relationship, and myself. I am loyal and I am fair. I love completely and without reservation, so helping Bart was not at all in question. My not helping Bart would have gone against the core of who I am and everything that I hold dear.

Sheree and Bart, photo by Sam Tyler

Chapter 8
THINGS I'VE LEARNED

Each stage of this ordeal was forging through new territory for the both of us. Our experience with the nervous breakdown or "crash" (as we often refer) was not something that came without warning. We just didn't know what these signs were telling us. His breakdown began quickly and rather blindly. This is not to say that Bart hadn't been acting differently and exhibiting signs of depression for some time. He had. Looking back, Bart had been under incredible stress for a long time. I should have seen it coming. His mother would ask about him periodically and I really didn't have an answer. I always tried to be optimistic, but I knew Bart's job was stressful and he always seemed convinced that he could handle it.

This brings me to a point that is necessary to make. Bart and I have always trusted and respected each other's role in our relationship. With that being said, Bart has never told me how to care for the children or run the household. He simply respected me, supported me, and trusted my judgment. Conversely, I have never told him how to run his business or do his job prior to this situation. I did express my opinion about some of the decisions he was making in the business that would directly impact our family, and even though sometimes his decision would go against my better judgment, I **always** supported him, respected him, and trusted his judgment. It was never my place to overstep my bounds and do his job too. I already had plenty on my plate. Besides, I never thought that was necessary. I trusted Bart. He knew it. I told him and I showed him. Do I really trust him if I go behind him on all of his responsibilities and try to help him do it my way, fix it, or re-do it? I don't think so. I have never wanted him doing that to me and he hasn't.

Nonetheless, we weren't prepared for what was happening and didn't have any idea what to expect in the future. We found ourselves strictly living in

the present. The only area in which we were certain was that we intended to fight for our relationship, **regardless**. And that is what we did.
We worked very hard in this capacity, but when we found circumstances to be too much, we didn't wait around. We visited with Boyce. Each of the visits that I or the two of us together had with Boyce was a turning point in the recovery. I highly recommend seeking out a qualified professional if you find yourself in a situation even remotely similar. These sessions provided clarity and helped to frame the issues at hand.

As time moves farther away from the breakdown, life has happened in such a way as to allow me glimpses of the struggles Bart was facing. I have experienced sadness, anxiety, and depression. I have experienced the struggles and frustration of trying to collect a check and all that this entails. I want to stress the fact that these glimpses are strictly that—just glimpses of what he experienced. They were merely opportunities to stand in Bart's shoes and look through his eyes, and regardless of how much I thought that I understood, I was wrong. I recently apologized to him for not seeing this so much sooner. There is much more clarity and perspective for me when reviewing his behavior surrounding the crash. I have so much more sympathy and empathy regarding his feelings. I know now what I couldn't understand back then. Bart was doing his best.

As the caregiver, you take so many licks that go unnoticed yet are felt so deeply on so many levels. They are not intentional. They are the effects of depression. I would liken it to dealing with someone who is suffering from drug addiction in this way. There are times when you are dealing with the drugs, not the loved one that has been taken over by this force. This thought helped me keep things in perspective in the midst of all of the trouble. When I looked at Bart, he didn't even look like the same person. Bart is a man who supports a 6'0", 220 lb frame. He has keen senses and an innate physical strength. He is a former collegiate baseball player who possessed the talent, determination, and drive to set records on each level of play. He is a man who grew up fishing and hunting where he developed a true love for the outdoors. This is who he is, and I say that in the present tense. The depression had taken over temporarily. During this time, he had a hollow look on his face and his body resembled a shell. He was weak and fragile, and his drive and determination had disappeared.

One facet of being a caregiver is not only the extent to which you feel emotion related to you, but also the pain that is experienced when watching a loved one in agony. We have all been there. It comes with the territory when being a parent. Actually, it is part of life and a chance you take when loving anyone. I am not at all minimizing the agony of the one suffering from depression because it is by far a beast with deep, piercing effects. It is also a condition that affects everyone around the depressed person. As the caregiver, I experienced a hurt and a fear like no other as Bart endured his breakdown. He was helpless, and it broke my heart. I think it was probably that hurt and fear that motivated me the most to push Bart like I did. I wanted to push him away from the depression, and I was so afraid that if I stopped pushing, I would lose him. It was as if depression was this huge, dark, bottomless abyss, and Bart had just teetered over the edge, and I had a white-knuckled grip on only one limb. It was all I had, and during the first two days, that is what I was doing—pulling him out of the hole. The rest of the time I was pushing him as far away from the pit as possible.

Bart, after his breakdown, during depression

Chapter 9
A COUPLE VISITS WITH BOYCE

The visits that I had with Boyce were extremely beneficial, but I have to say that the ones that were the most significant and memorable were the first visit in which he helped me see my value to Bart and one of the last ones. The visit which I am referring to involved a visit with both Bart and me. This visit came later on as Bart's recovery was progressing. He was doing better. There was still a long way to go, but we had made a significant move from the crash. Actually, at this time Bart was doing better emotionally than I was, but in all honesty we both were just a step above surviving.

It's funny how life works and how time helps perspective. When everything began to unfold with Bart, there was so much information to process and so many emotions to absorb. It was beyond overwhelming, somewhat similar to groping through a maze in a fog. His character traits are what prevailed for him, which encouraged my forgiveness. On an intellectual level, I had truly forgiven Bart, accepted the circumstances, and remained determined to move forward with him. However, on an emotional level, I was far behind. I hurt. I was sad. I felt betrayed regardless of what my head was telling me. I was mad. I was broken-hearted seeing Bart in such agony and yet so frustrated with him when he expressed no patience for my emotional struggles after he was in a more progressed state.

Emotionally, Bart had made progress because he had finally come to the point where all that he was running from and hiding from me had been revealed. I had forgiven him, and he felt more secure that our relationship would stay intact. For me, I had truly forgiven him with all that I could at the time. I could say it, mean it, and believe it. He deserved it. Intellectually, I had moved on. I emphasize—**intellectually**. Emotionally, it was an entirely different ballgame. I would have episodes where my emotions would take over and I would be so angry and my hurt would surface. At this point, however, I hadn't considered the intellectual and emotional differences and that this was causing a problem. I was feeling extremely out of balance in that when I was not strictly, directly focusing on a plan of action and pursuing it, my emotions would overtake me.

I remember an argument that Bart and I had one night. I don't remember how it began. What I do remember is that I was so irrational, and I could see it, which made the situation even more frustrating. For me, it was one of those experiences when you are actually participating in the activity and feel that you are viewing it as a spectator at the same time. Bart didn't hesitate to make the point that I was irrational and his frustration was that I shouldn't be acting that way because I had forgiven him. He was right and I knew it, but I was having issues that were real.

I remember during the argument he stormed out and called Bruce. Bruce told him that he had better just take it and listen because I had already put up with a lot out of him. I talked to Bruce as well. I don't know if it was in that conversation or in a future one that I was expressing my confusion and frustration about my feelings, and he made the point that intellectually I had forgiven Bart, but emotionally I wasn't there yet. I needed to heal. This was so enlightening and made so much sense. This had not dawned on me before. I had been hurt, really hurt, and Bart wasn't acknowledging it. In his eyes at this time, I had forgiven him, so he couldn't understand why I was having the emotional trouble. We have an understanding in our home that when something is settled, it is settled. We fight fair. This was exactly my problem. I had been functioning for so long only on the intellectual level because, as I said before, I had been Bart's emotional barometer which limited me addressing any emotion with Bart. Intellectually, I could move on and put it behind me. Emotionally, it was beyond my control. This only made me angrier at everything. Basically I was mad because my emotions were all over the place, and I was losing control. We were definitely at a point where this would have to be addressed. This led to another visit with Boyce.

My first visit with Boyce followed an emotional overload that peaked on my birthday. This visit was prompted the same way. I had reached that point again, and I was more than ready to visit with Boyce. This session resulted in yet another considerable turning point in our relationship and recovery. Prior to this particular session, Boyce suggested that Bart and I both come when I called to schedule. He had asked about the trouble that I was having, and based on the circumstances he felt that this was necessary. When I said something to Bart about Boyce's suggestion, he was in favor. Actually, Bart was always in favor of any therapy with Boyce. Bart felt that Boyce understood him, and so far, after every time that I had visited with Boyce, our relationship, under the circumstances, improved.

When we arrived, Boyce wanted to visit with Bart first. They were in there for at least an hour. I was called in afterward and Boyce counseled with the two of us. He had explained to Bart the problem that I was having. He guided us in resolving the issue. This was something that I never envisioned us needing prior to the breakdown—guidance in resolving an issue. However, Bart and I both welcomed the help.

During our couple therapy, I was able to express what I was feeling, which was that I had been really hurt, and even though I had truly forgiven Bart, there were times when issues would arise that would bring that pain to the front along with anger because he had never acknowledged that anyone else had been hurt but him. Boyce explained to Bart the needs that a wife has, and that those needs weren't being met or were being put in jeopardy. We also determined ways to help me resolve this issue, which allowed me some space when an issue would arise. To this point, "whatever" would arise, and it would be in my face, and I wasn't allowed an opportunity to deal with my emotions. I was just supposed to handle it.

Once Bart realized what had been happening, he acknowledged my feelings. He was sincere and disappointed that this had been happening and he hadn't seen it. His acknowledgement made all of the difference. It took the sting away and helped me take a different approach in the future. It allowed me the opportunity to see the situation more from Bart's perspective which provided a better understanding of his actions. Interestingly enough, even though we weren't arguing about degrees of hurt or pain, Bart was able to see that he wasn't the only one who got hurt during this ordeal and that by acknowledging my emotions this in no way minimized all that he had been enduring.

This whole situation wasn't fair, which goes without saying. Life isn't fair, but what I had to have was my emotions validated, and that had to come from Bart. With that, I was almost immediately able to put the painful emotions in past tense. Throughout 2006, Bart would continuously comment about how his emotions were real, regardless of them being fact based. So were mine. That is what I needed to be fair. I felt that I deserved it. Actually, I had to have it to move forward.

After this session, Bart and I became more united in dealing with future situations rather than me pulling him through while denying any of my own emotions.

Chapter 10
CHOICES

While processing the events as they occurred in 2006, I struggled with the presentation of information that continued to keep our life in upheaval. It was imperative that emotions be suppressed for the time being. One of my mantras throughout that aided perseverance was to "deal with the facts and only the facts." This was essential because Bart was operating on an emotional level only, and as we all know, emotions change. The facts don't. For me this was the only way that we were going to get to the heart of this problem, repair it, and move on. I was determined that we would get to the other side and that the facts were the beginning of that journey. Band-aiding and emotional decisions had been going on for far too long, and they were only temporary. I was ready to get ourselves out of this nightmare, never to return. This does not mean that I was or am so naive in thinking that we would forever be problem free, never to deal with depression again. My push was to move us from this survival mode to a place where prevention was our focus.

Prevention is one of my strengths. I prefer to work in an area of prevention. This could be because extreme circumstances produce extreme decisions. Our actions become reactions, and I don't like being in situations such as these, so much so that I work diligently to educate myself in prevention. I am an advocate of total body health and practice a healthy lifestyle to maintain a balance in my life. This is all good and fine as long as you are away from the fire, metaphorically speaking. However, there are times when you wake up and there you are—in the midst of the storm or fire or whatever, and prevention goes right out the window.

Now I know that it probably seems that this would be a no-brainer (not the time for prevention), but not for me. As determined as I was, I made sure that we were re-establishing those things that would promote a healthy lifestyle. I provided rigid structure where Bart was participating in light exercise, eating right, receiving adequate rest and reading his Bible. In my defense, I think that it was because it was what I knew. There is no doubt that Bart needed these things, but he also needed much more, and it took a while to discover what I was dealing with and why. I guess the comfort was that I was doing something to help him or help him in helping himself until we got to the heart of the matter. I liken my decision-making process to parenting. You do the best you can at the time. Evaluate the facts and analyze the situation to determine the best decision to make.

This brings me to an important facet of being a caregiver and that would be choices. You know I said that I would "deal with the facts, and only the facts." Well, this is true, but what do you do with the facts? Again, I know that this seems like yet another no-brainer, but not exactly. For me often times facts were trickling in making my information inconclusive. I had to make choices that had a huge impact on our future without all of the information. For me it seemed that our lives had changed drastically overnight and might not ever move back in balance. Life as we knew it very likely would never be the same. For Bart this change was something that he had been pushing back for so long before it overtook him.

I have always loved the relationship that Bart and I have. We have so much fun together, but throughout our relationship, I can't remember one time thinking of wanting to go back to a different point in time in our relationship. There are fond memories that are special, and I am proud that we have them, but not where I want to exchange it for the present, because the present is usually just as special. I do remember the reality of the situation coming into focus, though. I remember thinking how much I wanted to go back to the way things were and the fear that they might not ever be the same. However, the true reality is that life is always changing and nothing is the same. This brought about a choice I made. I refused to let this fear cripple me. It motivated me tremendously. I had to face the fact that things wouldn't be the same, and I became determined that they would be better. I believed that they would be better. We were already on this path, and the only way to deal with this "beast" was to bow up and face it head on. This reveals a significant piece of my personality. I *chose* to face it—**head-on**. I did my best to determine what I was dealing with and what I could do to get past it. By doing something, I felt that I was taking charge of the situation so that the outcome would be more favorable. In this case, it was my responsibility, and I owed it to Bart.

Regardless of whether I took charge or not, as the caregiver I was faced with making decisions. You know we are all faced with choices in life, and most of the time the choices don't bear such an impact on our life or much less even our day. But when a loved one is suffering with depression, especially a spouse, every decision is a big deal. For me they ranged from Bart's healthcare and emotional well-being to our finances and child-rearing. Of course, I was acting solely because Bart was simply not capable of functioning in a decision-making capacity.

Early on I was well aware of the impact that my decisions could have. I always had a choice, and I knew that my decisions had power. I remember days after the crash that Bart had been by Bruce and Rachel's house with Bruce before Bruce took him to the doctor. Rachel called me after they left to offer her support. She commented on Bart's condition, and she went on to say that I was his whole world. It is that very statement that illustrates the level of responsibility and pressure surrounding Bart's recovery. I knew and felt the responsibility that was in my hands. I was aware of the consequences should I misstep. I was aware of the influence and power, and with it all, I wanted to find us on the other side of this situation with me deserving that position. So the choice that ultimately patterned the course of all choices thereafter was the choice that I was going to do whatever it took to get Bart well and get us through this. Every other choice was made in order to accomplish this ultimate goal.

As I said before, most of the time I did not have all of the information. This presented a choice. I took the facts that I had and did my best to focus beyond emotion to do what would move us closer to the goal. I will share with you what I mean. My mother-in-law and I have always had a good relationship. She has always been very good to me and always means well. She had the same fears about Bart's health as I did; however, Bart would put her in difficult situations which oftentimes were counterproductive and would require so much discipline on my part to set the emotions aside, deal with the facts, and give the benefit of the doubt. I was the one who had to be firm and consistent. I was the one who was bringing on Bart's panic attacks. I was the one taking a beating emotionally, and Patsy was where he was going when he wanted to compromise the restrictions with money and for a safe place to land which would result in regression.

She was also the one who was in the middle and picked up Bart when he took off and I didn't know where he was. He was putting her in a difficult situation and couldn't understand the problems that were occurring until his counselor explained the matter to him. For me, his going anywhere to anyone other than me, and sharing emotionally, was showing that I really wasn't the most important to him. He asked the counselor to repeat what she had said so that he could write it down. He came home and told me about the session. He read to me what he had written down, and he apologized. I remember him saying that when she said that, it made so much sense to him. He didn't realize what was happening. He was broken-hearted when he realized what he had been doing to me. It was not intentional.

One of the most difficult times for me to set emotions aside and do whatever it took to stay focused on the goal was when Bart had taken off and Patsy picked him up. It was not easy, but it was necessary. I think it was so difficult not only because of the reasons that I just mentioned, but also because of the high level of emotions already swarming concerning Bart. Had I allowed myself to get sidetracked with any of these emotions, we would still be having trouble.

Now obviously, I am proud that Bart was safe and that he was with someone that I trust, but once again, it was a struggle with the facts and logic. First of all, Patsy and I have never had trouble with our roles in Bart's life. She is a top notch mother. There is nothing in this area of Bart's life that is lacking that would need to be compensated by me, and I have to say that I am really proud of that. I didn't take Bart to raise. I took him as my husband. I actually benefit from the relationship that Bart has with Patsy. With that being said, she has always been very supportive and helpful. As a mother-in-law, she has gone above and beyond to ensure that she and I have a good relationship. It is because of all of these things that facts weighed in her favor.

I would like to say that I simply saw the situation for what it was and moved on without a hitch. Not so. With the help of therapy that I mentioned previously and the assistance of my father-in-law who helped explain to Patsy the strategy that was in place, we were able to stay on course.

Patsy has always wanted and will always want to have a relationship with her son. She will also want them to be able to communicate. She was not encouraging Bart to come to her in place of me, and in her defense, what mother is going to turn her child away when they are hurting and they come to you. Actually, she was the one throughout that kept telling Bart to talk to me.

A point that I would like to make is that I have never had a problem with Bart communicating with his mother or any other family member for that matter. Ultimately, we all wanted the same for Bart. We wanted him well. In this context though, anyone that Bart was putting in this situation was going to be a problem.

This brings me to two things that were essential in order to proceed in the course determined by the choices made. Those would be trust and communication. I had to trust in God because He was my direction. During this time, I prayed without ceasing. I remember at one point in this situation when I was at my emotional breaking point. It wasn't a breakdown like Bart was experiencing. It was more like emotional overload. I remember walking into our spare bedroom that was known as the purple room, and I fell to my knees, sobbing and I cried out, "Please help me." I know that this sounds a bit dramatic, but it is true. I was confident that God was the source for my answers, and regardless of the tremendous help that was provided by those so close to us, I still felt very alone.

I was strengthened by the support of the special people in our lives at this time. Within all of the struggles that we were facing, I made a choice that provided me with a valuable lesson for the future. That would be choosing to involve Bart's parents in helping Bart and me with his recovery. Even though this was a choice that came naturally, it was nonetheless made. And the lesson learned was the way that Bart's parents supported me. It didn't matter if they agreed with me. They trusted me. This meant so much because these are parents that have never *not* been involved in Bart's life. I can't imagine how hard it was for them to step back and allow me to take charge of Bart's life when he was in distress. Even though this was my responsibility, and we all knew that, and even though they don't ever overstep their bounds in our lives, Bart's health was in a serious state. I could see the tendency to overstep at this time and try to take over. They didn't do that, and at the same time, there was never a doubt that Bart was anything less than one of the most important people in their lives, and they wanted him well. Based on their behavior at this time I was empowered by the trust that I felt they had in me and the support that they showed. Without a doubt, their actions at this time served as a lesson learned for me.

Realizing that regardless of how much trust they may have in me, we had to communicate, and we did. Communication served many needs at this time. We seemed to work most effectively when I communicated directly with one of my in-laws. Early on my father-in-law was the one who was so helpful. He was not as emotional as my mother-in-law which was helpful for me. I would find myself more frustrated with Bart after talking with Patsy, and I didn't need any help at this time in that area. My father-in-law was also able to assist me with business dealings relating to the partnership. We worked well together. He has a knack for knowing just how to behave during a sensitive time.

It was after we had moved beyond the first stages where Bart was so fragile and his condition so uncertain that Patsy was most helpful. Life wasn't as emotional, and I simply needed her to do what a mom does.

Chapter 11
BEHAVIORS

A common question that I have been asked concerning Bart's crash is: What did he do; how did he act? So I wanted to share that with you. Having already described the onset of Bart's depression, and how he was before and after, you can see how depression can consume someone and turn them into someone that they aren't. I equate it to dealing with someone suffering with a substance abuse of some kind. Once that problem manifests itself and becomes active, you are dealing with the problem and not the person. But with any problem of this nature, it waxes and wanes, and we began to become aware of some of the signs.

Bart would be experiencing a period of progression, and it seemed without warning he would begin to slip. One significant behavior that surfaced was how Bart would slowly begin to withdraw from me. Our dialogue would become very superficial. This was a somewhat subtle change initially that would become rather pronounced as it progressed. In retrospect, I found myself dismissing this particular behavior as insignificant because of how subtle it was. Now it is a major red flag that forces me to act.

This withdrawal was primarily from me, because even though he was showing improvement, his interaction with others aside from work was slight for quite some time following the breakdown. It was just so much effort for him during this time, and this is something that I didn't push. Bart was already dealing with an overload of fear, and I was not at all encouraging anything more than what was necessary. Those situations made Bart very nervous and uncomfortable, so if they weren't necessary, we didn't do it. The fact that those he was around cared about him and were concerned was irrelevant. This fear was so big for him.

In my opinion, fear is the root of anxiety and depression. Actually, it seems out-of-control fear is the core. It is fear that feels so overwhelming that it becomes crippling. I don't think fear is a bad thing. Of course, I'm referring to a fear that is motivating and manageable. When our fear is within these parameters, it is a force that can drive us to do our best and be our best. With someone dealing with anxiety and depression, fear becomes that boulder that is squashing the life out of them. Because these victims have a fear that is unbalanced, they become frozen in this state. Bart was trapped in this fear. When this fear or helplessness became too great, he would suffer with a panic attack.

Bart's first panic attack occurred in our kitchen. His panic attacks were primarily fostered by my anger or anytime that I would press him on an issue that had to be addressed. He did suffer panic attacks that were triggered by others, but ultimately they all stemmed from a fear that was overwhelming. I would only press him when he was the only one who had the information that was necessary at that time. Otherwise, I dealt with it myself. When I got angry, this would bring Bart's fears too close to becoming a reality. So I did my best to suppress my anger until it would overtake me, and I would explode. Pressing an issue scared him. He was afraid that revealing whatever he could remember would in-turn make me angry and his fears would become a reality. Something that I want to point out is Bart's memory. Bart has a sharp memory. He can often recite conversations that we have had. This is unfortunate when we are discussing an issue that comes down to an order of events conversation and he is right. So when I say "whatever he could remember" I mean it. During the breakdown, his body had shut down, his adrenals were burned out, and his serotonin had been depleted which all aided in providing him with a chemical imbalance. His mind was in a fog as a result, and possibly for his own protection. He really could not recall specifics, details, or some events. This is something that I did not know or understand at the time. If I did know it, I wouldn't believe it because it just seemed impossible. But it was his true inability to recall that made so much of what he did seem dishonest.

Anyway, once a panic attack was prompted, it could not be stopped. When Bart had his first one, it really scared us both. They would begin with him gasping for air. He felt that his oxygen was being cut off. His fear didn't help with the situation. He couldn't be still. He would stagger around and fall on the floor. I would talk to him throughout if I was with him. I would remind him to breathe, relax, and try to be still. I had to remain calm in order to keep his fear from escalating.

When Bart had his first one, I remember thinking that this could possibly be a heart attack, but it just seemed that it had to be a panic attack because of the events preceding its onset. It seemed to last quite a while, but it was really only a few minutes. I found that with future panic attacks, the faster that I could get him to calm down, the shorter his panic attacks would be. After a panic attack, Bart would be relaxed and tired. As his recovery progressed, there were times when a panic attack was inevitable because an issue would arise that had to be addressed. I learned to be cautious but direct in presenting the issue.

It was probably June when I began to identify a new warning sign that was an indication of a stall in Bart's progress. His behavior would change, and he would become very clingy. This was a consistent behavior with Bart and still is a telltale sign of a potential depression bout. He was like this immediately preceding his breakdown. I remember asking him what he was doing. I had contracted the flu, and this particular strand had an incubation period of ten days minimum. Nausea was one of the symptoms with this flu. Bart hates to be nauseated. He will not get around or allow anyone in our house who is suffering with a stomach virus. He is helpful around the house when someone has it, but he will get prepared with anti-nausea medicine on hand.

At this particular time, he would follow me around and make himself susceptible to my symptoms. This didn't make sense at the time. I remember asking him if he was trying to get sick. So when June rolled around and this behavior appeared again, I started to put it together. Bart and I began to track it. It would occur in relation to collections and when bills were due. Since this was the source of Bart's anxiety, when this cycle would come around again, his fears would overwhelm him. Knowing this, we began to kick into high gear the prevention methods from before and do whatever was necessary to alleviate the impending anxiety.

Now I realize what you may be thinking. He was clingy and distant? Yes! He exhibited both at the same time. I found it frustrating initially, and I think that was because I couldn't pinpoint the problem. It just seemed like some arbitrary behaviors with no logical connection. However, by June when I noticed his clingy behavior returning, I started to pay attention. I was also able to see that during these periods, Bart was scared, and he needed a safe place. This was his primary thought, and it drove all of his actions. This fear drove him like intense physical pain would drive someone. At a time like that, the only thing that matters is finding relief.

Other symptoms that I have noticed with Bart when a depressive bout is looming is his appetite and sleep habits decrease significantly, which in turn bring about other health concerns. Bart never makes a big deal when he feels bad or when something is bothering him unless it is something between the two of us—this breakdown situation aside. Otherwise, he quickly dismisses any concerns about his eating or sleeping patterns. Without a change of some kind, this situation moves in a downward spiral. Because of all that has happened with his breakdown, I don't wait to confront him when I notice any of these behaviors starting to appear. I go straight to the heart of the issue. I can simply ask him what is bothering him, because I am noticing certain things that are indicative of on-coming depression. He is then usually very forthcoming in sharing his concerns.

Chapter 12
LIFE IS A GIFT FILLED WITH BLESSINGS

Life is a gift filled with blessings, don't you agree? I know that this may sound a bit odd after reading the struggles that we faced in 2006, but this is what I believe. Without a doubt, I would not want to go through those struggles again, so I am very diligent about ensuring that preventative

Bart, Todd, & Jenna feeding seagulls at the beach

measures are taken. However, I do believe that it was during this time that we were blessed more than we realize and for that I am so very thankful.

A common phrase that comes to mind when I reflect on 2006 is: "It is in the valleys that we grow." I can't take credit for that. It was shared with me by Bart's grandmother during this time as words of encouragement, and I can't begin to count the number of times that I have thought of it since. It is so very true. Do we realize our potential? I discovered so many things about myself. I found myself in many circumstances that are not what I would consider my comfort zone. There were areas where I would normally rely on Bart that became my responsibility, and I had to find a way to make it work. My true priorities rose to the top, and I found a new confidence in my abilities. But most importantly, my faith in God grew. I trusted Him. I knew that I didn't know what I was doing or what I was facing, but I knew where to go and that was to Him in prayer. In the middle of all the turmoil, it was really the only way I found any peace. God was my guide.

Another blessing that I found was simply living in the moment. I realize that many of you already know this, but for me this can be an area where I struggle. I have to consciously focus on the act of staying in the present, because I am a high energy level person and driven to complete my goal. This is not to say that you cannot do both. I simply tend to fol-

Sheree, with Sandy

low my natural tendencies which do not naturally include both, although the circumstances occurring in this year forced me to do more of that, and oftentimes it was grueling. However, one day that was rather special and for which I was extremely thankful was Mother's Day 2006.

Mother's Day was after my birthday and after the incident of Bart's disappearance. We were on the pendulum swinging back the other way. We didn't get out of bed all day. I was so drained and I hurt all over, but Bart and I were getting along like we had in the past. I remember that we watched an Andy Griffith Show marathon. It was as if this was a brief moment in time where we were not focusing on the past or anticipating the future. We were strictly in the present, and it was just us. Our children were playing well together and doing their own thing. From a business standpoint, the banks were closed. Nothing could be done on this day. I have to think that at a time like that, a day like that was truly a gift. We were in the present, and it was awesome.

Another time that brought about a new level of gratitude was around the holidays. I have always been one who is excited about the celebrations and anxious to see my children as they find their presents left by Santa, but this year was different. Gratitude took on a whole new meaning. It was as if I was so aware

Jenna and Sheree at the Toad Suck Race

Todd's first day of school

of my blessings and amazed at how far we had come. Just a few short months prior I didn't dare look beyond the present. With the past year being as it was, I have had to entertain circumstances that were far from favorable. But from those circumstances came growth and increased strength for which I am thankful. My greatest gift this year and every day since has been all five of us having our health and being together. I know—how cliché. But it is true. It only takes one time of facing a potential life altering situation to completely diminish the commercialism of the holidays and allow you to face each day with new appreciation.

Heaviness is yet another blessing that comes to mind. Yes, you read that correctly. It was the feeling that I didn't think would ever go away, and yet I had forgotten it until recently when I heard a story on the news of someone whose current health condition was dismal and the future was promising to be a struggle. Even though their struggle was not what we had faced, I was saddened because I was confident that they are dealing with the same "heaviness" feeling. In fact, I feel that any intense struggle that lasts over a period of time will be accompanied by "heaviness."

I remember waking in the morning and my first thoughts were—I'm awake, I'm alive, and with a heavy sigh, the nightmare continues. This does not mean that I was not thankful for being awake and being alive. I was and am very much so. It was the nightmare bearing so much weight. We couldn't wake up from it. We couldn't ease the pressure. We just had to sigh and keep putting one foot in front of the other. What is interesting about this heaviness feeling is that neither of us realized how heavy it really was—how it was affecting every area of our being until we began to see glimpses of relief and I began to deal with the health issues brought about by the intense stress.

Obviously, Bart was dealing with health issues prior to his crash and thereafter, but my health issues began to develop during the summer following the breakdown in March. The stress that we had been dealing with had completely thrown my body out of sync and had me facing chronic health conditions. The irony to this, though, was that as frustrating and uncomfortable as the health issues were, and initially it seemed to be adding even more issues to address, for the most part it was a diversion. Bart and I were at a new place regarding his recovery at this time. We had an improved strength at this point. I had a new beast to slay. Bart and I were on the same side, and it was refreshing. I had the support that I needed, and we persevered.

Now the reason that I am thankful for the heaviness is without the heaviness, I would never be able to see the depth of the blessings. After all, how do you know how good something is until you see how bad it could be? And how do you know what you're made of until you're put to the test? Don't get me wrong. I am most thankful that the heaviness of this situation is no longer bearing down, but it did at one time, and I am willing to learn what I can from it. Most certainly, it is that we are blessed.

Finally, I am thankful for the events that have occurred since Bart's breakdown which enable me to understand him more and more. These opportunities allow me to identify with Bart and his circumstances at the time so much better. I continue to be in awe at his strength.

I hope for you that you are encouraged by our story and that you find the strength to persevere through whatever challenge life brings your way. I don't speak with all of the answers. I just share what we faced and what we did. What I would like to leave with you is motivation to see your choices and the realization of the impact of the decisions that follow. My advice would be to always seek to learn all that you can, love with all you have, and trust God in everything. I would also like to leave you with two passages that always give me comfort especially in times of struggle.

Trust in the Lord with all of your heart, and lean not on your own understanding; in all your ways acknowledge Him and He shall direct your paths. Proverbs 3:5-6

For He Himself has said, "I will never leave you nor forsake you." Hebrews 13:5

I HOLD YOUR HEART IN MY HANDS

I hold your heart in my hands with loving, gentle care. It was given to me completely, without reservation—*the greatest of all honors.* I will always love it as my own. My hope is that I will always be all that you could ever want, need, and desire.

I hold your heart in my hands, providing it more support than it requires. My hope is that this support will provide you complete courage and confidence necessary to achieve all that this heart desires.

I hold your heart in my hands, protecting it from all harm, danger, and deceit. I stand ready to fight and defend it on all fronts, never allowing opportunity for so much as a negative thought to reach its exterior. By doing so, I hope to eliminate avoidable sadness and grief from your life.

I hold your heart in my hands, with great honor and respect for the responsibility which is before me. I cautiously preserve your dignity everywhere with everyone, realizing that a man's dignity begins with his wife. My hope will forever be that others see you as I do.

I hold your heart in my hands, striving to provide a lifetime of happiness through love, laughter, and complete joy. My desire is that you will always be able to look at our life with a smile on your face.

I hold your heart in my hands, always seeking those opportunities to affirm your security and trust. By doing so, I hope to give you the peace necessary to face all of life's experiences.

I hold your heart in my hands, recognizing the power that I possess. With this fragile, special element, I have the ability to mold and influence our future. I hope to make a difference by always putting the well-being of this heart in my hands before my own. I hope to be the example that I should be so that you always desire the life that is pleasing to the Lord.

I hold your heart in my hands, hoping to provide the comfort that is needed when situations seem unbearable. I hope to ease the bruises and help endure the pain when circumstances overwhelm. I will see you through it.

I love you, your heart, and everything about you.
Sheree

This analogy occurred to me one day while I was running. I wrote this for Bart as soon as I came in from the run. This is my role and my responsibility in our relationship **always**.

A family photo, fall '08. by Sam Tyler

More Bible workbooks that you can order from Spiritbuilding.com or your favorite Christian bookstore.

BIBLE STUDIES

Inside Out (Carl McMurray)
Studying spiritual growth in bite sized pieces

Night and Day (Andrew Roberts)
Comparing N.T. Christianity and Islam

We're Different Because..., with Manual (Carl McMurray)
A workbook on authority and recent church history

From Beneath the Altar (Carl McMurray)
A workbook commentary on the book of Revelation

1 & 2 Timothy and Titus (Matthew Allen)
A workbook commentary on these letters from Paul

The Parables, Taking a Deeper Look (Kipp Campbell)
A relevant examination of our Lord's teaching stories

The Minor Prophets, Vol. 1&2, w/PowerPack (Matthew Allen)
Old lessons that speak directly to us today

Esteemed of God, the Book of Daniel (Carl McMurray)
Covering the man as well as the time between the testaments

Faith in Action: Studies in James (Mike Wilson)
Bible class workbook and commentary on James

The Lion is the Lamb (Andrew Roberts)
Study of the King of Kings, His kingdom, & His return

Church Discipline, with Manual (Royce DeBerry)
A quarter's study on an important task for the church

Exercising Authority, with Manual (John Baughn)
How we use and understand authority on a daily basis

Communing with the Lord (Matthew Allen)
A study of the Lord's Supper and issues surrounding it

Seeking the Sacred (Chad Sychtysz)
How to know God the way that HE wants us to know Him

1st Corinthians & 2nd Corinthians study guides (Chad Sychtysz) *Detailed studies to take the student through these important letters*

TEENS/YOUNG ADULTS
Transitions, with PowerPack (Ken Weliever)
A relevant life study for this changing age group
Snapshots: Defining Moments in a Girl's Life (Nicole Sardinas)
How to make godly decisions when it really matters
The Path of Peace (Cassondra Givans)
Relevant and important topics of study for teens
The Purity Pursuit (Andrew Roberts)
Helping teens achieve purity in all aspects of life
The Gospel and You (Andrew Roberts)
13 weeks of daily lessons for Jr High and High School ages
Paul's Letter to the Romans (Matthew Allen)
Putting righteousness by faith on an understandable level

WOMEN
Reveal In Me... (Jeanne Sullivan)
A ladies study on finding and developing one's own talents
I Will NOT Be Lukewarm, with PowerPack (Dana Burk)
A ladies study on defeating mediocrity
The Gospel of John (Cassondra Givans)
A study for women, by a woman, on this letter of John
Sisters at War (Cassondra Givans)
Breaking the generation gap between sisters in Christ
Will You Wipe My Tears? (Joyce Jamerson)
Resources to teach us how to help others through sorrow
Bridges or Barriers, w/Manual (C. DeBerry & A. Kmitta)
*Study encouraging harmony between younger/older
sisters-in-Christ*
Learning to Sing at Midnight (Joanne Beckley)
A study book about spiritual growth benefiting women of all ages
Forgotten Womanhood (Joanne Beckley)
*Workbook which covers purity of purpose in serving God as a
woman*

PERSONAL GROWTH
Compass Points (Carl McMurray)
22 foundation lessons for home studies or new Christians
**Marriage Through the Ages, with Manual
(Royce & Cindy DeBerry)**
A quarter's study of God's design for this part of our life
**Parenting Through the Ages, with Manual
(Royce & Cindy DeBerry)**
Bible principles tested and explained by successful parents
What Should I Do?, with Manual (Dennis Tucker)
A study that seeks Bible answers to life's important questions
When Opportunity Knocks, w/PowerPack (Matthew Allen)
*Lessons on how to meet the Jehovah's Witness/
Mormon who knock on your door*

SPECIAL INTERESTS
In the Eye of the Hurricane - AUTISM (Juli Liske)
A family's journey from the shock of an autistic diagnosis to victory
**I Cried Out, You Answered Me - DEPRESSION
(Sheree McMillen)**
What happens when faith and depression live in the same home
Her Little Soldier - DIABETES (Craig Dehut)
The journey of a young man suffering from Juvenvile Diabetes
For However Brief a Time (Warren Berkley)
A son's human interest tales of his father in a time now gone by
**Family Bible Study Series, with Curriculum Guide
(Ken Weliever)**
16 quarters of Bible class curriculum for families and congregations

***All PowerPacks include PowerPoint presentations +
Teacher's Manual**